Lecture Notes in Operations Research and Mathematical Economics

Edited by M. Beckmann, Providence and H. P. Künzi, Zürich

5

L. P. Hyvärinen

IBM European Systems Research Institute Geneva

Information Theory for Systems Engineers

1968

Springer-Verlag Berlin · Heidelberg · New York

All rights reserved. No part of this book may be translated or reproduced in any form without written permission from Springer Verlag. © by Springer-Verlag Berlin · Heidelberg 1968.
Library of Congress Catalog Card Number 68-28758. Printed in Germany. Title No. 3755.

PREFACE

This book is based on lectures given by the author at the IBM European Systems Research Institute (ESRI) in Geneva.

Information Theory on the syntactic level, as introduced by Claude Shannon in 1949, has many limitations when applied to information processing by computers. But in spite of some obvious shortcomings, the underlying principles are of fundamental importance for systems engineers in understanding the nature of the problems of handling information, its acquisition, storage, processing, and interpretation.

The lectures, as presented in this book, attempt to give an exposition of the logical foundation and basic principles, and to provide at the same time a basis for further study in more specific areas of this expanding theory, such as coding, detection, pattern recognition, and filtering.

Most of the problems in Appendix C are intended as extensions of the text, while calling for active participation by the student. Some other problems are direct applications of the theory to specific situations.

Some problems require extensive numerical calculations. It is assumed in those cases that the student has access to a computer and that he is capable of writing the necessary programs.

The student is assumed to have a good command of the calculus, and of the theory of probability as well as statistics. Therefore no basic mathematical concepts are discussed in this book. The Fourier transform and some related mathematical concepts are introduced in Appendix A.

The author is indebted to Dr. G. M. Weinberg and Dr. H. Tzschach of ESRI for their valuable assistance and contributions in the writing of this book.

Geneva
January 1968
Lassi Hyvärinen

CONTENTS

Capter 1

    Introduction

        1.1 Properties of Information   1

        1.2 Levels of Information   2

        1.3 Information Media   7

        1.4 Reversible and Irreversible

                      Processes   8

PART I

Capter 2

    Noiseless Channels

        2.1 Character Set and Channel   12

        2.2 Channel Capacity   15

        2.3 Information Content, Entropy   17

Chapter 3

    Coding for Noiseless Channels

        3.1 Decision Tree   25

        3.2 Example of Coding and its

                      Efficiency   28

        3.3 Optimum Codes   35

        3.4 End of Message Condition   45

        3.5 Decipherable and Instant Codes   48

Chapter 4

    Joint Events, Natural Languages

        4.1 Joint Events   51

        4.2 Conditional Information   56

        4.3 Natural Languages   64

Chapter 5

    Noisy Channel

        5.1 Channel Matrix and Information Rate   72

        5.2 Capacity of Noisy Channel   77

        5.3 Ideal Observer   82

Chapter 6

    Error Checking and Correcting Codes

        6.1 Hamming Distance, Parity Checking   88

        6.2 Error Correcting Codes, Hamming Bound   94

        6.3 Some Other Redundancy Codes   101

PART II

Chapter 7

    Properties of Continuous Channels

        7.1 Continuous Signals   105

        7.2 Sampling and Desampling   107

        7.3 Gaussian Noise   112

        7.4 Entropy of Continuous Information   115

7.5 Information Rate and Channel Capacity   119

Capter 8

Detection of Continuous Signals

    8.1 Principle of Ideal Observer   124

    8.2 Reception of Steady Voltage in Noise   129

    8.3 Correlation Reception   134

Chapter 9

Information Filters

    9.1 Convolution Filter   145

    9.2 Real-time and Off-line Filters   154

    9.3 Filtering Redundant Time Series   157

References   164

APPENDIX A

    Fourier Transform and Related Concepts   166

APPENDIX B

    Binary logarithms and Entropies   184

Appendix C

    Problems   185

INDEX   202

CHAPTER 1

INTRODUCTION

1.1 Properties of Information

What do we understand intuitively by "information"? A message, a sound pattern, a page of a book, a TV image, the outcome of a physical measurement.

What common properties of the above examples are characteristic of information?

a) In order to convey information, the contents of the message or the outcome of the measurement should be <u>unknown</u> to the receiver <u>before</u> reception. A message whose content is known to you before you have read it does not transfer information.

This property can be expressed in other words: There must be more than one possible sequence of symbols (pattern or numerical value) before reception. At the reception this <u>uncertainty</u> is removed and the choice is narrowed down to one particular sequence.

b) In order to receive "true" information, we might require, further, that the receiving person can understand the <u>meaning</u> of the message. Thus, for example, a message in an unknown language or a ciphered message without the key would not constitute information.

c) A further property, we might impose on information, is that the message were relevant to the receiving person. That is, it has **value** or he can **use** the information for a decision or for initiation of an action.

1.2. Levels of Information

We can define, in terms of the above properties a)- c), three different aspects or levels of information:

        a) syntactic
        b) semantic
        c) pragmatic

1.2.1. Syntactics

On this level of information we are mainly interested in the number of possible symbols, words or some other suitable elements of information, their durations, statistical and deterministic constraints of successive symbols imposed by the rules of adopted language or coding system. Further, the syntactic information theory is a study of information carrying capacities of communication channels and the design of appropriate coding systems for an efficient data transfer with high reliability. No attention is paid to whether the information has meaning or practical significance.

Limited as it is in its scope, information theory on the syntactic level is of high applicability in data communication and data processing. This is because the mode of operation of information media such as telephone, telegraphy, television, radar, telemetry, and teleprocessing networks is independent of the meaning and significance of the transmitted data. In data processing some of the application areas are, for example, data compression techniques, error checking and correcting codes, sampling and smoothing of time series, data prediction.

In all subsequent chapters the word "information" is used to mean only syntactic information unless stated to the contrary.

1.2.2 Semantics

Great difficulties are encountered when trying to define semantic information in exact mathematical terms. This is, in part, due to the fact that it is to a greater extent dependent on the receiving system (person) than the syntactic information. For example, the understanding of a message depends on whether the receiver has the deciphering key or not, or whether he understands the language.

The problems in automatic language translation are almost exclusively of semantic nature.

Another area of data processing involving semantics is information retrieval. The most successful systems today are based on the concept of key words. The technique is satisfactory in scanning scientific and technical articles and their abstracts. This is due to the relatively precise and inambiguous use of technical terms. However, different authors and scientific diciplines have not come to an agreement of a standard terminology and probably never will.

In addition, context and association of words (symbols) play an important role in semantic problems, even more so in the normal every day use of language. Besides, a word in the semantic sense is a label or symbol that has been given a meaning and is, therefore, always a matter of convention, variable with time and environment and defying the rules of formal logic.

1.2.3 Pragmatics

On the pragmatic level of information we are concerned with the value or utility of information, which is necessarily even more a function of the receiver than was the case in semantics.

The pragmatic content of information depends strongly on time.

Consider a management information system in a manufacturing

company. The system is providing at regular intervals, or at request, reports on production, sales, inventories, etc. In addition to syntactic and semantic information in these reports, they contain also pragmatic information to the management. The information has value and utility if right and timely decisions can be based on them.

If, however, the reports are late, their value will be decreased. Thus, the utility of information is a function of the time elapsed from the event to the reception of the report.

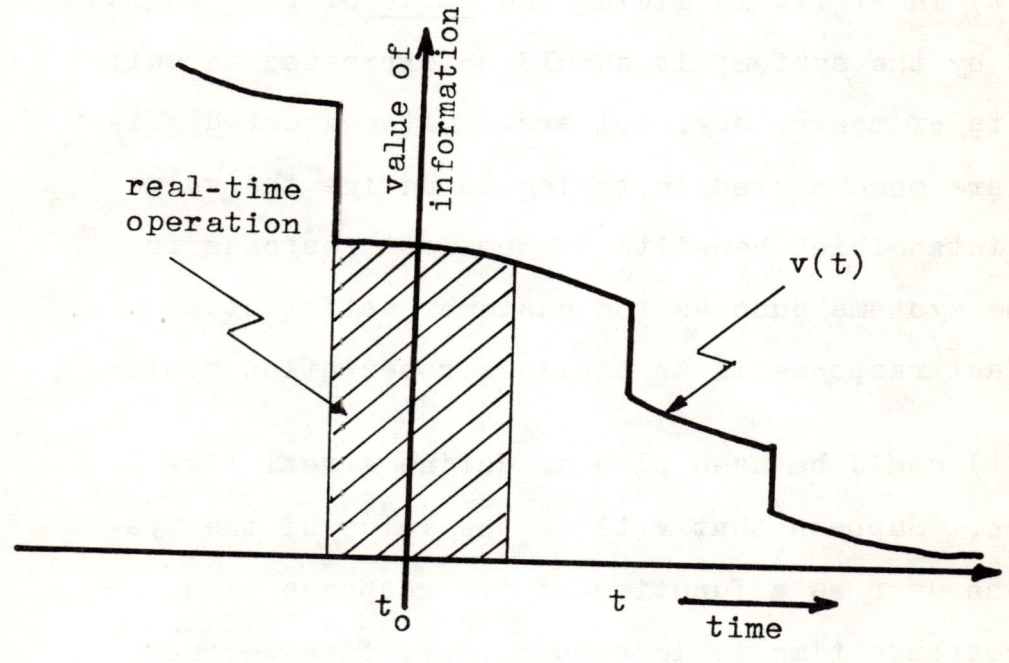

Fig. 1.

This is a non-increasing monotonic curve of the type depicted in Fig. 1. Time t_o is the instant the event ocurred. The pragmatic information or value, $v(t)$, may have discontinuities at points corresponding to some critical dead lines.

In the domain $t < t_o$ the information of the event is available before it occurs, i.e., prediction. Obviously, this information, if equally accurate and reliable, will have even higher pragmatic value.

Ultimately, in any information system, it is the pragmatic information that the user is willing to pay for. More complex and expensive real time systems can be justified only by the increased utility of fast response information over off-line systems.

Since $v(t)$ in Fig.1. is giving the <u>value</u> of information provided by the system, it should be expressed in suitable units of money, say, dollars. Often great difficulties are encountered in trying to define the value of the "intangible" benefits of the fast response in real time systems such as the customer satisfaction of the fast response in an airlines reservation system.

Curve $v(t)$ could be used also to define a real time operation. Suppose that $v(t)$ is the value of the system to the user as a function of the response time. If the response time is less than, say, five seconds it is still as good as if it were five milliseconds. That is, there is a "plateau" of $v(t)$ with sufficiently small response times. This plateau can be defined as the region of real time operation.

1.3. Information media

On the syntactic level of information we may say that information is stored or transmitted in any medium that can assume more than one distinct state in space and/or time.

A printing position on a page of a book can take on in English 26 distinct alphabetic characters (ignoring different styles of type and capital letters), space (blank), ten numerical digits, and a number of special characters and punctuation. These are the possible _states_ of a printing position.

A ferrite ring in a computer core memory will be only in two distinct magnetic states.

A band limited sound pattern of finite duration can take on a finite number of wave forms with given power limitations and finite resolution of the receiving equipment. Each of these distinct wave forms can be understood as a state of the medium.

Other media of information: traffic signs and traffic lights, measuring instruments, TV image (black and white or color), Morse dots and dashes, combination of a safe, strings of genes and chromosomes.

If the medium where information is stored or transmitted can be divided into discrete units in space or time and each of these units, or cells, has a finite number of possible states (a character in a printed message, the state of a ferrite ring etc.) we have a <u>discrete</u> information system. Digital data processing systems are discrete.

If such a basic information cell cannot be uniquelly defined we have a <u>continuous</u> information system. Examples: non-digital measuring instrument such as a voltmeter, pitch and amplitude of a sound wave, color and brightness of a graphic pattern, field strength of a radio emission.

Continuous signals can be made discrete (digitized) without loss of information by sampling techniques, but the sampled signal is not uniquely determined by the continuous signal (phase of sampler).

Whether the system is discrete or continuous is often a matter of convention. For example, a printed page is considered discrete with distinguishable printing positions and a finite number of available characters. But the same medium (paper) could be used for storing continuous type of information such as a grey tone picture.

1.4. Reversible and Irreversible Processes

Consider a source of information (a printed page). Let this information be processed in a certain way (for example translated to another language). Let us call this process A. The output of process A gives the source information in a new form. If it is possible to find another process, B, that can reproduce the source information exactly in its original form we call process A <u>reversible</u>. See Fig. 2. If no such process B exists we call process A <u>irreversible</u>. (It is assumed that after the transformation A no reference can be made to the source information.) Obviously, process B, when it exists, is reversible.

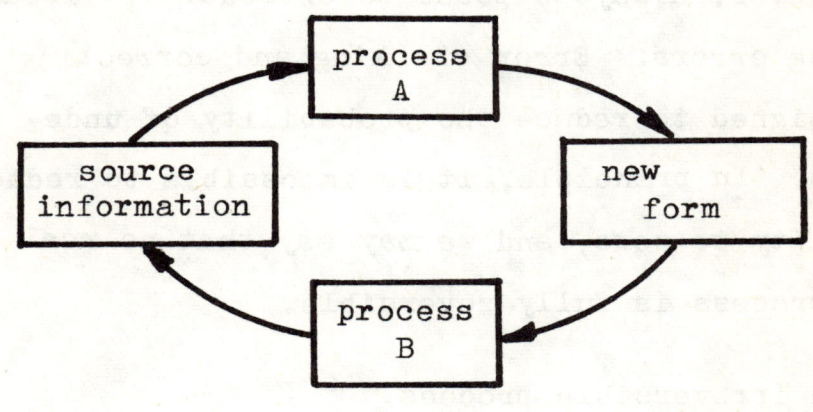

Fig. 2.

A reversible process retains all information contained in the source information; an irreversible process destroys a part or all of the information.

A translation process of a natural language is in most cases irreversible. If we take a simple sentence such as "He is a man" and let some one translate this into German: "Er ist ein Mann", we get a unique translation. If this sentence is given to another person for a translation into English the probability is very high of getting the original sentence assuming that the two translators have a sufficient knowledge of these languages. But if we have a whole book to translate the probability of reversible translations is infinitesimal.

Data coding is an information process that is designed to be as closely reversible as possible. Data being processed in a computer or transmitted over communication lines is, however, always exposed to external disturbances generating errors. Error checking and correcting codes are designed to reduce the probability of undetected errors. In principle, it is impossible to reduce this probability to zero, and we may say that no real information process is fully reversible.

Example of an irreversible process.

Assume that the source information consists of an array of 250 numbers representing the daily sales of a store during a calendar year. Process A consists in computing the average daily sales, the variance and the trend. These three numbers are the "New form" of information.

Evidently, this process is highly irreversible since the 250 source data cannot be reproduced from the three numbers. Most of the source information has been destroyed by the process.

Is this, then, a reasonable way of handling information?

A computer system is often used to distill or filter out of a wealth of "raw" source data a few <u>significant</u> parameters and, perhaps, to store the source data in a retrievable form for future reference.

By processing the data the computer can never generate new information that was not already in the source data. It can transform it into another form and at best maintain it, given that the process is reversible.

An irreversible process is a selective information filter that may increase its <u>utility</u>, for example, in decision making. In this case the computer is increasing the <u>pragmatic</u> information.

Similarly, an appropriate processing may give <u>meaning</u> to the information, meaning that was not directly observable in the source data, even though it was contained in it. (See L. Brillouin, Chapter 19.)

PART I

DISCRETE INFORMATION SYSTEMS

CHAPTER 2

NOISELESS CHANNELS

2.1. Character Set and Channel

A discrete information system, such as a written natural language, utilizes a finite number n of different symbols (letters, characters) $S_1, S_2, S_3, \ldots, S_n$. We shall call the ensemble S_j, $j = 1, 2, \ldots, n$ the character set. The words "character" and "symbol" are used interchangeably.

Ignoring numerals and punctuation the English language has a character set of 26 letters and the word space or blank. Consequently n = 27 for this set.

..., t_n we have, also, fixed the information carrying properties of the channel.

The definition of the character set S_j, as such, is not unique. For example, in a written natural language, we may select the letters as the basic elements or symbols. Instead, we could consider a word as the basic unit and define S_j as all the words in the dictionary. Clearly, in this case we would have a variable length character set.

In a teleprocessing system the S_j could be considered as the collection of all possible (formated) messages with respective lengths t_j.

The symbols S_j may be, also, considered as "states" of the channel. Thus, if we have in some particular position of the medium, or information cell, a symbol S_j, we may say that the cell is in state j. (See 1.3.)

In information storage and communication the messages are exposed to disturbances that may change the character, say, from state i to state j, with a non-zero probability $p_i(j)$. This __uncertainty__ in the received or detected symbol is called __noise__.

No real information channel is completely free of noise. Therefore a noiseless channel theory pertains to a fictitious idealization. There are, however, cases where the noise is negligible and since the noiseless case helps develop some basic ideas, we shall take it first under detail study.

Also, no distinction is made in this simplified form between capital and low case letters.

Each character S_j occupies a certain space along the printing line. We shall denote this by t_j. In data communication t_j is, respectively, the duration of character S_j. Thus, in general t_j is the amount of the medium required for the storing or transmission of S_j.

If t_j is constant for all j the character set is fixed length, otherwise we have a variable length character set.

This typewriter is an example of fixed length character set. Same applies to line printers in computer systems. Electric typewriters and type setting machines utilize variable length characters using, for example, less space for an "i" than for an "m". The Morse code is variable length, whereas computers use coding systems with fixed length "bytes" or "words".

In the noiseless case (for noise see below) the information carrying properties of the medium are completely determined by the character set S_j and the associated durations t_j. These together constitute what is called the information channel or simply the channel.

That is, as soon as we have selected the symbols $S_1, S_2, \ldots, S_n$ and the durations (or space requirements) $t_1, t_2,$

By this token, we can define

(2) $$C^{(m)} = k \ln(M_m) = k\, m \ln(n)$$

as the <u>information capacity</u> of a noiseless channel with a set of n symbols of constant (unit) duration and m positions or cells. k is a coefficient of proportionality which will be determined immediately. ln(n) is the natural logarithm of n to the base e.

Due to the additive (linear) relation to m, we can express the channel capacity $C^{(1)} = C$ per cell

(3) $$C = k \ln(n)$$

For n = 27   C = 3.30 k.

The simplest possible channel is the binary channel with S_1, S_2 and n = 2. For this case we have by (3)

(4) $$C = k \ln(2)$$

By convention, C for the binary channel is defined as the unit of channel capacity, or k = 1/ln(2). By substitution of this in (3) we get

(5) $$C = \ln(n)/\ln(2) = \log_2 n = \log n$$

where $\log_2 n$ is the logarithm of n to base 2 (binary logarithm). In order to simplify the notations we are going to use notation "log", without the base, to indicate the binary logarithm.

2.2 Channel Capacity

For the purpose of deriving some of the basic concepts of a noiseless channel, we consider first the case that all n symbols S_j have the fixed duration $t_j = t = 1$. As a specific case to carry the ideas through, consider, further, that the channel consists of the letters of the English alphabet plus the blank character, each using a unit printing position. Thus, $n = 27$.

In order to define the information capacity of the channel, we first express the number M_m of possible different messages that can be printed on a page, say, of m printing positions. Since each position can take on one of the n characters we have obviously

(1) $$M_m = n^m$$

We would accept, intuitively, as a measure of information storing capacity of the page, some monotonically increasing function of M_m.

Another intuitive requirement is that the capacity of two pages should be twice that of one page. That is, the function should be additive with respect to m.

The logarithmic function has both of these properties. And it turns out to be the most suitable definition in other respects, too.

Expression (5) is a dimensionless number, but when used to measure information we call the unit "bit".

For the English alphabet

$$C = \log 27 = 4.76 \text{ bits/letter}$$

If the constant duration $t_j = t \neq 1$ is also taken into account

(6) $$C = \frac{1}{t} \log n$$

where C now is expressed in bits per second or bits per line millimeter or equivalent.

The case of variable length symbols will be covered in section 3.3.

2.3 Information Content, Entropy

We have used for the definition fo the information capacity of a given channel the logarithmic measure of the number of possible combinations of n symbols in a sequence of m positions. Similarly, in principle, we could define the information content $I^{(m)}$ in a string of m symbols in terms of the number N_m of acceptable messages that actually would occur.

Apparently, if we are dealing with a natural language only a small percentage of the M_m possible sequences (Equation (1)) would ever occur. Thus,

(7) $\quad N_m \ll M_m = n^m$

Consequently, the information content, if defined as the logarithm of N_m would be less than the capacity.

(8) $\quad I^{(m)} = \log N_m < m \log n = C^{(m)}$

Same applies for the information content per cell

(9) $\quad I < C$

We can write

(10) $\quad N_m \leq n^{m'}$

where m' is the smallest integer satisfying (10).

Then, it would be possible, in principle, to associate each acceptable sequence (message) of length of m characters with a unique combination of m' characters. This process of assignment is a coding process that compresses the original data in less space. Further, we could set up a dictionary containing all the pairs of original and compressed messages. By this means the coding process is reversible and no information is lost. One possible coding procedure would be to arrange the N_m messages and the $n^{m'}$ code sequences in the alphabetic order and match them one-to-one.

Coding systems of the above type are commonly used in data processing. Take, for example, the spare part inventory of a repair shop. The names of the spare parts are often dozens of letters long. By assigning them appropriate numeric or alphanumeric codes each of them can be identified by a reasonably short sequence of characters. The coding and decoding processes are table look-up programs.

Summarizing: We were able to store the information in a sequence of m characters of original message, without loss, in a channel capacity less than $m \log n$. The channel capacity required per character of original message is

(11) $$C' = \frac{m'}{m} \log n < C = \log n$$

Is (11) the least possible capacity where the information can be stored without loss?

Suppose that we have found the minimum capacity C_{min} in which the information can be coded reversibly. This capacity could be defined as the information content. This method would be analogous to defining the amount of, say, water as the volume of the smallest bucket that can hold all the water without spilling over.

The coding process resulting in C_{min} will be called the optimum code.

Optimum coding schemes will be discussed in Chapter 3. It will be seen that in most cases the optimum code is based on variable length code words, based on the relative frequencies (probabilities) at which each character or group of characters occurs.

In the special case that all acceptable messages N_m (Equation (7)) occur at <u>equal frequencies</u> the minimum capacity C_{min} and the <u>information content</u> are given, at the same time, by expression (8). This statement, which will be used in the derivation of the entropy expression below, will not be proven here, but it is easily accepted by the following simple arguments:

1) The proposed code of m´characters is the shortest possible fixed length code.
2) There is no basis for a variable length code since all messages appear alike to the channel, which pays no attention to the actual contents of the message, due to the uniform frequency.

The unit of information content is "bit", the same as for the capacity.

The <u>information rate</u> I is defined as the information content divided by the number m of characters in the original sequence. Its unit is bits/character, bits/line millimeter, bits/second or equivalent.

Entropy:

Assume that in a long sequence of m binary characters, say, $S_1 = A$ and $S_2 = B$ ($n = 2$), we have always exactly m_1 characters A and m_2 characters B. ($m_1 + m_2 = m$) Then the number of possible messages N_m is the combination

$$(12) \qquad N_m = \frac{m!}{m_1! \, m_2!}$$

If it is, further, assumed that all of these different sequencies occur at the same frequency (at the same probability) we can write the information content of the sequence by (8), (12) and the statement on page 20

$$(13) \qquad I^{(m)} = \log N_m = \log m! - \log m_1! - \log m_2!$$

Since it was assumed that $m \gg 1$, we can use the asymptotic formula of the logarithm of a factorial

$$(14) \qquad \ln m! = m(\ln m - 1) \qquad m \gg 1$$

Thus, assuming that also m_1 and m_2 are high numbers

$$\ln N_m = m(\ln m - 1) - m_1(\ln m_1 - 1)$$
$$- m_2(\ln m_2 - 1)$$
$$= m \ln m - m_1 \ln m_1 - m_2 \ln m_2$$

The latter form is obtained by applying the equation $m = m_1 + m_2$. Since, now, every term has a natural

logarithm, it is valid for binary logarithms, too.
By applying again equation $m = m_1 + m_2$ and dividing through by m

$$(15) \quad I = \frac{I^{(m)}}{m} = \frac{m_1}{m} \log(m/m_1) + \frac{m_2}{m} \log(m/m_2)$$

If we let m grow indefinitely, the ratios m_1/m and m_2/m can be interpreted as the probabilities p_1 and p_2 at which the two characters S_1 and S_2 occur in a typical message. Further, the assumption that every sequence with m_1 A's and m_2 B's occur at equal probabilities implies that successive symbols are statistically independent.
Hence, (15) may be written

$$(16) \quad I = -p_1 \log p_1 - p_2 \log p_2$$

The same approach applied to an arbitrary number n of characters S_j results in similar expression

$$(17) \quad I = -\sum_{j=1}^{n} p_j \log p_j = H$$

This expression is called the <u>entropy</u> of the probability distribution p_j and denoted by H.

Summarizing: The <u>information rate</u> of a noiseless channel of character set S_j ($j = 1, 2, \cdots, n$) of constant durations $t_j = 1$ and probabilities p_j of occurrence is equal to the entropy of the distribution p_j provided that successive characters are statistically independent.

By the assumption of statistical independence the actual numbers m_j of characters S_j in the sequence of length m would not be exactly mp_j but distributed according to the multinomial distribution. That is, the actual number N_m of possible sequences would be higher than (12), and, therefore, one would expect the information rate I to be more than the entropy (17). But, now, the possible sequences are no longer equiprobable and application of the fixed length code m´ does not generate the minimum storage capacity.

It can be shown that by applying an appropriate optimum code of variable length the minimum capacity will lead to an information rate equal to the entropy.

The case of statistical dependence between successive symbols and its effect on the information rate will be analyzed in Chapter 4.

An important property of entropy (for a proof see, for example L. Brillouin, pp. 14-17) is that it assumes the maximum value when all p_j are equal

$$(18) \quad H_{max} = -\sum_{j=1}^{n} \frac{1}{n} \log(1/n) = \log n$$

$$\text{for } p_j = \frac{1}{n} \text{ ; all } j$$

By comparing (18) with (5) we notice that

$$(19) \quad H_{max} = C$$

The maximum information rate equals the channel capacity and it is achieved only if all characters of the character set occur independently at the same frequencies.

Entropy is a measure of the <u>uncertainty</u> of the contents of the message before it has been received. If we assign a character the "surprise value" equal to $-\log p_j$ we are rewarded by this amount at the reception of S_j. As the fraction of these reward cotributions is p_j the mean surprise value in a long sequence is the sum of $-\log p_j$ weighted by teir probabilities or exactly the entropy.

Notice, that if we know the next symbol in advance with certainty, p_j for this S_j is equal to 1 and zero for all the others. For this distribution the entropy is zero, that is, no information is received if there is no àpriori uncertainty.

This case represents, at the same time, the minimum entropy. That is, $0 \leq H \leq \log n$.

Notice, also, the important property of the entropy that its value is independent of to which particular characters S_j the given probabilities p_k are assigned as long as the same numbers are used in some permutation.

Further properties of the entropy are analyzed in later chapters as needed.

CHAPTER 3

CODING FOR NOISELESS CHANNELS

3.1 Decision Tree

Consider a noiseless channel with n = 3, $t_j = 1$, where the three characters S_1, S_2, and S_3 are statistically independent with probabilities p_1, p_2, and p_3, $(p_1+p_2+p_3 = 1)$. The information rate per character is by (17)

(20) $$I = -\sum_{j=1}^{3} p_j \log p_j = -p_1 \log p_1 - p_2 \log p_2 - p_3 \log p_3$$

The process of receiving a symbol of a message can be represented by the upside down tree of Fig. 3., in which each branch represents a possible outcome after the symbol has been received.

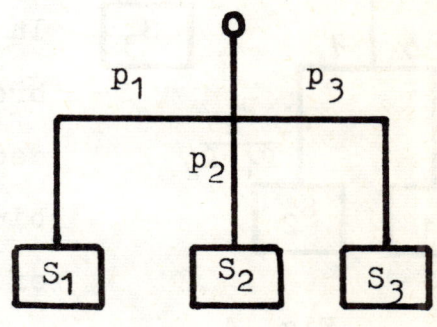

Fig. 3.

The same process can be split up to two successive stages of decision. Suppose that the possible outcomes are first dividen into two subsets (S_1, S_2) and (S_3). At the first stage we are given the binary piece of information that the symbol is in the first (code = 0) or the second (code = 1) subset. The probability of a 0 is p_1+p_2 and of a 1 respectively p_3. In the latter case this piece of information is enough for us to know that the symbol is S_3.

If the outcome of the first decision is zero we continue by further dividing the subset (S_1, S_2) in two subsets of the next level (S_1) and (S_2). This sequential decision process is given a graphic interpretation in Fig. 4.

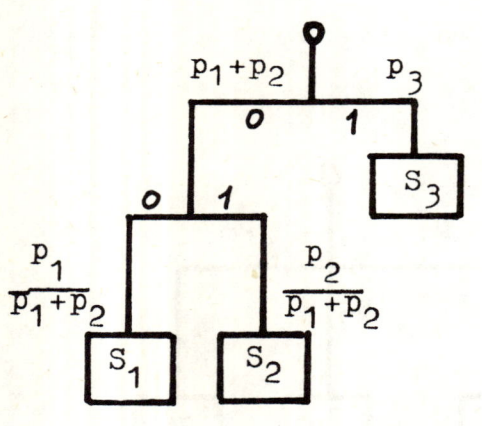

Fig. 4.

In this example we have broken the original n-ary decision into a series of binary decisions. The series of outcomes of the decisions generates a binary code of the original character set of n characters. Thus, in the above example the binary code of variable length would be

$$S_1 = 00, \quad S_2 = 01, \quad S_3 = 1$$

If we divide the character set at each stage into k subsets the ensuing <u>decision tree</u> generates a k-nary code for the n-ary character set.

Let us find the mean information content of the first decision stage in the example above.

$$I_1 = -(p_1+p_2) \log(p_1+p_2) - p_3 \log p_3$$

The probabilities of a zero and a 1 at the second stage, when needed, are $p_1/(p_1+p_2)$ and $p_2/(p_1+p_2)$, respectively. The information at this stage is the the entropy of this binary distribution weighted by the probability (p_1+p_2) that it will occur.

$$I_2 = -(p_1+p_2) \left[\frac{p_1}{p_1+p_2} \log(\frac{p_1}{p_1+p_2}) + \frac{p_2}{p_1+p_2} \log(\frac{p_2}{p_1+p_2}) \right]$$

The total mean information content of a binary <u>code word</u> of the code at the bottom of the previous page is the sum I_1+I_2. It is readily verified that this sum is equal to the entropy (20). This means that the total information in the two decision trees of Fig.3 and Fig.4. are equal.

The mode of reception represented by Fig.3. is "parallel" reception where the whole character is given in one dose. Fig.4. is a "serial" receiver getting each character in successive steps.

The concept of the decision tree is most useful in the analysis and design of coding schemes and optimum codes in a noiseless channel. The same approach will be used later, also, when discussing the conditional information in the case that successive symbols are not statistically independent.

3.2 Example of Coding and its Efficiency

The following example is intended to illustrate the dependence of the information rate on the coding system in a given channel and the use of the decision tree.

Assume a binary channel (n = 2) with $S_1 = 0$ and $S_2 = 1$. Further assume $t_j = 1$ and symbols statistically independent with $p_1 = 5/6$ and $p_2 = 1/6$. Following sequence of 35 characters was generated by throwing a die, and it may be considered a representative sample of a long message.

...00001000000000001000100100000001000...

The channel capacity

$$C = \log n = 1 \text{ bit/character}$$

The mean information rate with given p_j is

$$I = -(5/6) \log(5/6) - (1/6) \log(1/6) = 0.647$$

With m = 35 we have respectively for the sample

$$I^{(35)} = 35\ I = 22.65 \text{ bits}$$

$$C^{(35)} = 35\ C = 35 \text{ bits}$$

The ratio of the information content to the used capacity of channel is defined as the <u>coding efficiency</u> E. This is a dimensionless number ranging from zero to one.

(21) $$0 \leq E = I^{(m)}/C^{(m)} = I/C \leq 1$$

For our example and the original sequence of symbols

$$E = 0.647$$

Our problem is to find a coding scheme that would be reversible and reduce the capacity requirements.

Looking at the sample sequence we are struck by the rareness of the 1's, and we would expect to reduce the length by just indicating the locations of these symbols.

To do this, let us try the following method: Divide the sequence in five groups of seven binary characters each. Indicate the positions of the 1's within a group by octal numbers 001 to 111. Indicate the end of a group by the octal zero 000. The sample sequence is then transformed into

... 101 000 000 011 111 000 011 000 100 000 ...

The spaces between the octal numbers are not necessary and they have been added only to improve readability.

This code is certainly reversible and, therefore, has the same information content 22.65 bits. But the capacity used has been reduced to 30 bits from 35. If this can be considered as a good estimate of the mean capacity in a long sequence the coding efficiency for this code is

$$E \cong 22.65/30 = 0.755$$

which is an improvement over the original message.

Next, let us try to be more systematic by applying the concept of the decision tree.

Since the binary character set does not easily lend itself to this we increase the character set to $n' = 16$ by considering a group of four consecutive binary characters as a new symbol. The new set S'_j consists of the 16 four digit binary numbers 0000 to 1111. In order to have complete groups we increase the sample to $m = 36$, the next binary symbol being a zero. Thus,

... 0000 1000 0000 0000 1000 1001 0000 0001 0000 ...
    S'_1 S'_9 S'_1 S'_1 S'_9 S'_{10} S'_1 S'_2 S'_1

Successive characters being statistically independent the probabilities p'_j of the new symbols S'_j are readily calculated from the binomial expression

$$p'_j = p_1^k p_2^{n-k}$$

where $p_1 = 1/6$, $p_2 = 5/6$ are the original probabilities of the characters S_1 and S_2, and k is the number of 1's in S'_j.

j	S'_j	p'_j	w_j code word	t'_j length
1	0000	.4823	0	1
2	0001		100	3
3	0010		101	3
5	0100	.09645	110	3
9	1000		1110	4
4	0011		1111000	7
6	0101		1111001	7
10	1001		1111010	7
7	0110	.01929	1111011	7
11	1010		1111100	7
13	1100		11111010	8
8	0111		11111011	8
12	1011		11111100	8
14	1101	.00386	11111101	8
15	1110		11111110	8
16	1111	.0008	11111111	8

Table 1.

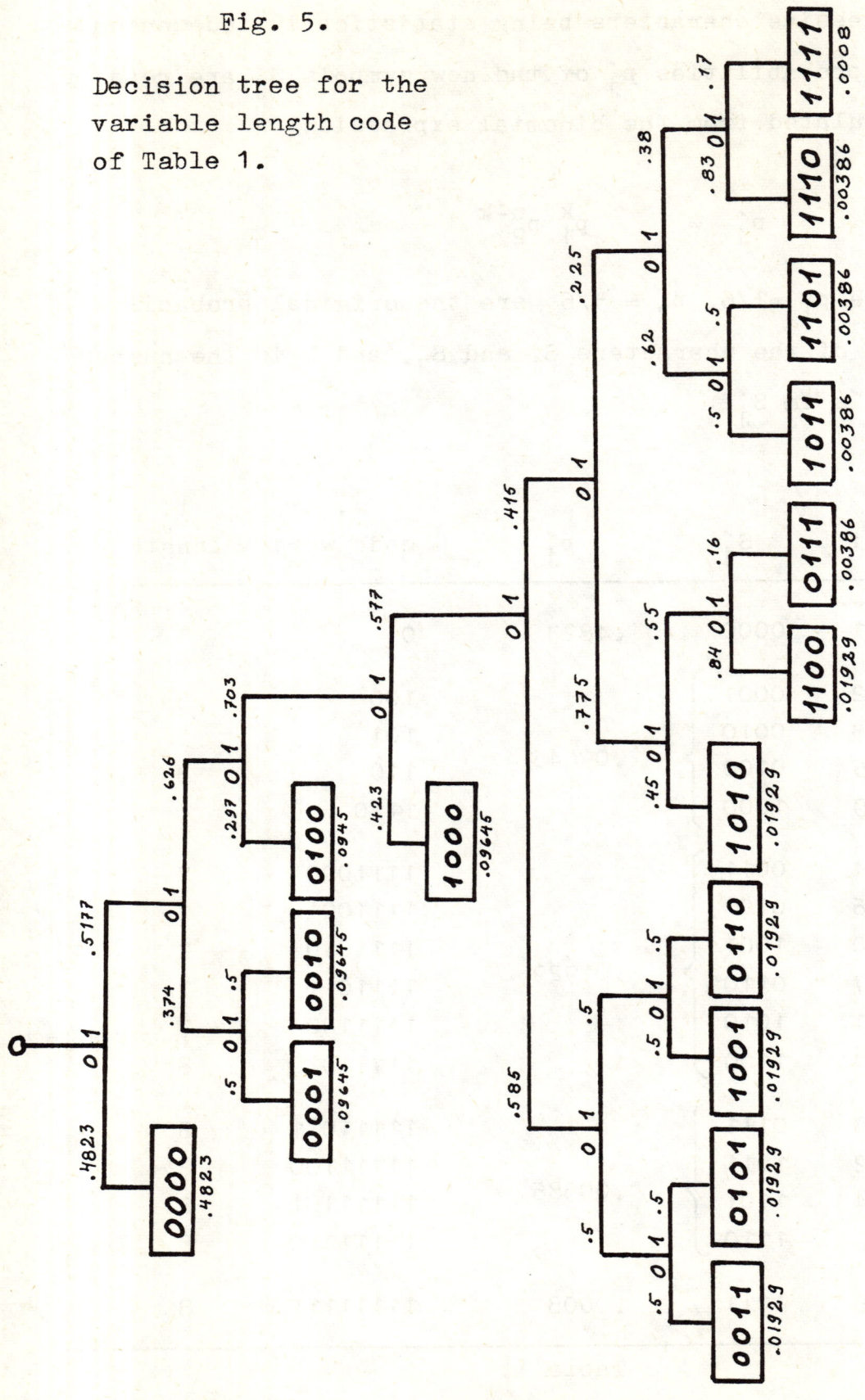

Fig. 5.

Decision tree for the variable length code of Table 1.

The numerical values of these probabilities are given in Table 1.

In order to design a binary code for S_j' with the highest possible information rate we should try to find a decision tree with well balanced probabilities of the two branches at every stage. If we succeed to have exactly equal probabilities in the whole tree the information gained at every stage is one bit, and the information rate equals the channel capacity. This would be an optimum code with coding efficiency $E = 1$.

Fig.5. on the preceding page is the result of a trial and error effort to find a well balanced decision tree. The figure contains probabilities p_j' and of going to the left or right at each stage. It can be seen that in most of the cases these probabilities are quite close to ½.

Designing a balanced decision tree has some common features with building a mobile.

The variable length wode words w_j and their lengths t_j' have been carried from Fig.5. to Table 1.

In this coding, the sequence of the 36 original characters (bottom of page 30) is reduced to (spaces added for readability.)

... 0 1110 0 0 1110 1111010 0 100 0 ...

The capacity used for the sample sequence is 23 bits. The information content of this sequence of 36 original characters is $36 \times 0.647 = 23.3$ bits. Thus the coding efficiency becomes

$$E = 23.3/23 = 1.01$$

This result seems to refute the theorem that the information rate cannot exceed the channel capacity. It should not be forgotten, however, that this holds exactly only for the means of very long sequencies. The information rate in the above calculation is the mean obtained by the entropy, but the capacity pertains only to a short sample and is, therefore, only an estimate of the mean.

What is the mean channel capacity requirement of this code?

This can be computed from the data in Table 1. The mean number of bits per S'_j is, obviously, the sum of the lengths t'_j weighted by their probabilities p'_j.

$$C = \sum_j t'_j \, p'_j \quad \text{(bits/code word)}$$

From the data of Table 1. it is found that $C = 2.70$. As this is the capacity per four original symbols the actual coding efficiency becomes

$$E = \frac{4 \times 0.647}{2.70} = 0.96 < 1$$

3.3 Optimum Codes

The optimum code, as already mentioned, is one having a coding efficiency E equal to one, that is, the information rate equals the channel capacity.

It has become apparent from our coding examle that a high coding efficiency requires that the most frequent symbols (S_j') should be assigned the shortest code words, and for the rare symbols we can accept longer code words.

In the following we are going to develop some more exact conditions for an optimum code. There are very few equations in coding theory to serve as a recipe of design. Most of the relationships that can be established are inequalities being necessary but not sufficient conditions. They provide, however, useful guidelines in the design of optimum or nearly optimum codes.

First, we are going to derive an important inequality of the entropy expression.

Consider the following expression for K.

(22) $$K = \sum_j p_j \log q_j \quad ; \quad \sum_j p_j = 1$$

where p_j is the probability of the symbol S_j and the q_j are a set of n non-negative numbers such that

(23) $$\sum_j q_j = Q \leq 1$$

Let us write the q_j in terms of the p_j that have been given a "correction" term x_j.

(24) $$q_j = p_j + x_j = p_j(1 + x_j/p_j)$$

Then the x_j satisfy the condition

(25) $$\sum_j x_j = Q-1 \leq 0$$

By substitution of (24) in (22) we have

(26) $$K = \sum_j p_j \log\left[p_j(1 + x_j/p_j)\right]$$

$$= \sum_j p_j \log p_j + \sum_j p_j \log(1 + x_j/p_j)$$

The following inequality is easily verified for any real y.

(27) $$y \geq \ln(1+y) = k \log(1+y)$$

$$k = \ln(2)$$

The equality in (27) holds only for $y = 0$.

We apply this to the second term of (26) with $y = x_j/p_j$.

(28) $$K \leq \sum_j p_j \log p_j + \frac{1}{k}\sum_j p_j(x_j/p_j)$$

(28) (cont)
$$K \leq \sum_j p_j \log p_j + \frac{1}{k} \sum_j x_j$$

Or, by substituting (22) for K and using (25)

(29)
$$\sum_j p_j \log q_j \leq \sum_j p_j \log p_j + (Q-1)/k$$

On what condition do we have equality in (29)? By replacing the logarithms in the second summation of (26) by x_j/p_j we can only increase the right hand side. In case of equality this increase should be zero for <u>all</u> terms of the summation, or, by (27), all x_j should be zero. This implies $q_j = p_j$ due to (24) and $Q = 1$.

This being the only case of equality, we obtain finally by reversing the signs and taking into consideration that Q-1 is non-negative (25)

(30)
$$-\sum_j p_j \log q_j > -\sum_j p_j \log p_j$$

given that $\sum_j q_j \leq 1$ and not all $q_j = p_j$

Next, we shall apply this inequality to a variable length binary coding scheme such as in Paragraph 3.2.

Consider a variable length binary code with n code words S_j of lengths t_j or a channel with an n-character set S_j and durations t_j. As in the example of Paragraph 3.2, we can write the mean capacity per code word or character, assuming independent probabilities p_j of occurrence for the symbols

$$(31) \qquad C = \sum_j p_j t_j = - \sum_j p_j \log(2^{-t_j})$$

The information rate per symbol is the entropy

$$(32) \qquad I = H = - \sum_j p_j \log p_j$$

By considering $2^{-t_j} = q_j$ and assuming

$$\sum_j q_j = \sum_j 2^{-t_j} \leq 1$$

we have by (30)

$$I = - \sum_j p_j \log p_j \leq - \sum_j p_j \log(2^{-t_j}) = C$$

The equality $I = C$ or the coding efficiency $E = 1$ is possible only if

$$(33) \qquad \sum_j 2^{-t_j} = 1 \quad \text{and} \quad p_j = q_j = 2^{-t_j} \quad \text{for all } j$$

Condition (33) can be expressed also as

(34) $$t_j = -\log p_j$$

Equation (34) is a **necessary** and **sufficient** condition for an **optimum code**. It does not, unfortunately, tell us how to design the code words to meet this condition.

We can write from (31) and (32) a general expression of the coding efficiency of a variable length channel or code.

(35) $$E = \frac{-\sum_j p_j \log p_j}{\sum_j p_j t_j}$$

If we reconsider the variable length code proposed by the decision tree of Fig.5. and given in Table 1. we find that the first condition (33) is satisfied. In general $\sum 2^{-t_j} = 1$ for any decision tree with no "open ends", that is, every branch ends in a valid code word. If the tree has at least one open end the sum $\sum 2^{-t_j} < 1$. Thus, we may apply (34) to every code generated by a decision tree.

Further, it is seen that we can have an optimum code only if the tree has no open ends.

How well is condition (34) satisfied in the code of Table 1?

It can be seen that the actual lengths t'_j of Table 1. are in a fairly good agreement with the lengths of the optimum code in Table 2.

p_j	$-\log p_j$
.4823	1.05
.09645	3.37
.01929	5.70
.00386	8.00
.0008	10.10

Table 2.

Notice, that, for example, three of the four code words of probability .09645 have length $t'_j = 3$ and one the length 4 resulting in an average of 3.25, which is reasonably close to the 3.37 of Table 2.

In the (discrete) binary coding we are restricted to code word lengths that are integral multiples of a bit of capacity. In principle, though, the lengths can be non-discrete for a given channel, for example, the spaces taken by letters in a manual type setting.

If we are using a k-nary decision tree with k branches at every stage to generate a k-nary code it can be shown by the same approach as above that the optimum code conditions become

$$\sum_j k^{-t_j} = 1$$

(36) and

$$t_j = -\log_k p_j$$

where $\log_k$ is the logarithm to base k.

A k-nary decision tree with a constant length (duration) of the k coding elements (such as 0 and 1 for the binary code) generates code words whose lengths are integral multiples of this element. Let us denote by N_t the number of code words whose length is t times the elementary length. These numbers N_t cannot be chosen arbitrarily and independently since they are limited by the structure of the tree.

We shall derive, next, an inequality expressing this restriction.

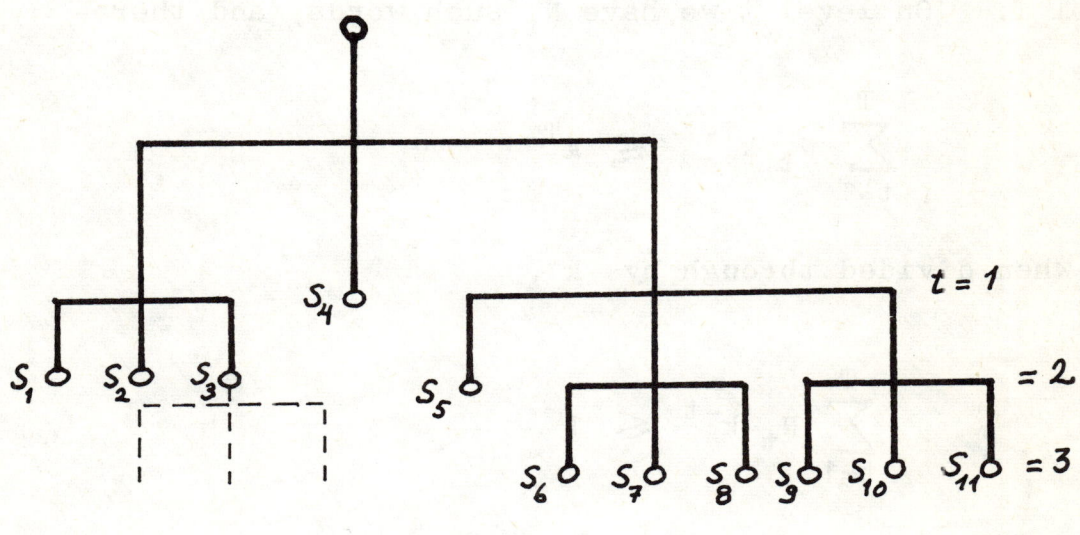

Fig. 6.

Fig. 6. is an example of a ternary tree (k = 3) with a maximum code word length $T = t_{max} = 3$.

Obviously, if all code words were of the maximum length T = 3, we would get a set of n codes with $n = 3^3 = 27$.

Or, in general,

(37) $$n = k^T$$

possible code words, where T is the highest t for which $N_t > 0$.

A code word of length t represents a branch of the tree terminating on level t. This particular branch, if continued to the last level T, would cover k^{T-t} code words of those in (37) (see Fig. 6.). Hence, such a code word is using up k^{T-t} terminations on level T. On level t we have N_t such words, and therefore

$$\sum_{t=1}^{T} N_t \, k^{T-t} \leq k^T$$

Or, when divided through by k^T,

(38) $$\sum_{t=1}^{T} N_t \, k^{-t} \leq 1$$

Let us apply this condition to our coding example. Table 2. gives the optimum code word lengths for the case of Table 1. We also notice that there are respectively 1, 4, 6, 4, 1 code words with equal probabilities. So, the nearest thing to do, would be to round the optimum lengths of Table 2. to the nearest integer

In this case $k = 2$, $T = 10$.
Table 3. gives the suggested N_t and terms
$N_t k^{-t}$. We see that
the sum (38) is geater
than one and, therefore,
this code is not possible.

t	N_t	$N_t 2^{-t}$
1	1	1/2
3	4	4/8
6	6	6/64
8	4	4/256
10	1	1/1024

sum = 1137/1024

Table 3.

Again, condition (38) can be used for a quick check whether a suggested code is at all possible, but it does not indicate how to modify the code to get at the same time a most optimal and possible code.

We see in Table 3. that the two first rows ($t=1$ and $t=3$) already add up to one. Hence, we must reduce N_3 to 3 and move one code word to a higher t. By such a trial and error method we can arrive in a distribution of N_t that make (38) exactly equal to one.

Equality in (38) corresponds to the case that there are no open ends in the decision tree, that is same as the first of conditions (33).

Is the coding system of Table 1. the nearest optimum there is? No. It is, in principle, possible to get E arbitrarily close to 1 by systematic iterations. We are going to mention some of them, but even using the groupings of four (S_j') of Table 1. it is possible to design another binary code that has a higher coding efficiency than 0.96 found so far. It is left to the reader to find it by applying methods developed in this paragraph.

One of the systematic approaches is known as the <u>Shannon-Fano method</u> (see for example L. S. Schwartz, pp. 16-19). This is a binary coding method that can be described by the decision tree.

Let the original character set be S_j, $j = 1,2,...,n$. with probabilities p_j. The characters are arranged in a sequence of decreasing probability and divided into two subsets so that we start picking up characters from the higher end of probabilities to the first subset until they add up to as closely as possible to ½. The remaining characters make up the second subset. This division, then, determines the first binary branch and the first code digit 0 or 1.

The two subsets are further divided in the same way, until all S_j have a unique binary code.

If the resulting code has a high enough coding efficiency, the process is stopped there.

If the code is not efficient enough, we proceed as follows.

All n^2 possible ordered pairs $S_j S_k$ are defined as the new character set with probabilities $p_j p_k$ in case of statistical independence of successive characters. The same process of division into binary subsets and code assigning is applied to this new character set as to the original. Since we, now, have a wider selection of probabilities it can be expected that the binary decisions are more evenly balanced giving a higher coding efficiency.

The same method is applied to triplicates, quadruples, and so on until the code meets the efficiency requirements.

Note, that in Paragraph 3.2. we are utilizing ordered quadruples of the original binary characters as S'_j, but the decision tree is not based strictly on the subdivision by descending probabilities.

Another systematic method for optimum coding, that should be mentioned, is the **Huffman code**. We are not going to describe it here but the reader will find a detailed description, for example, in R. B. Ash, pp. 40-43.

3.4 End of Message Condition

Different coding methods such as the Shannon-Fano code are based on groups of a suitable number of basic characters. The message length is not always exactly a multiple of the group. This happened in the example of Paragraph 3.2 where we had to comlete the sample message from 35 characters to 36 in order to get a multiple of four.

Let us assume, first, that the binary channel has in addition to the two character states 0 and 1 an idle state. States 0 and 1 could be two distinct carrier frequencies and the idle state a silent channel.

In this case, the end condition can be indicated by an incomplete code word, something like in Table 4.

incompl. code w.	meaning
none	last group complete
1	omit last digit
11	omit 2 last digits
111	omit 3 last digits

Table 4.

If we have such an idle state the channel is, in fact, ternary ($k = 3$), and to use the third state only for the indication of the end of the message is wasteful. A considerably more efficient code could be designed by using the idle state also for character coding.

Assume, next, that the channel has no additional idle state to make an incomplete end condition code possible. Now, what we need is four complete code words, one for each end condition. These can be understood as "special characters" or "control characters" and they should be included in the decision tree in a position corresponding their frequencies in normal use. The "blank" character in a written text is such a control character, the period (.) and other punctuation serve a similar purpose.

We find in computer coding a number of control characters of this type. They are called "word marks", "record marks", "end of message characters", or many other names. Certain computer codes provide an additional bit, the flag bit, just for the purpose of indicating the end of a data field (variable field length computers). This seems like a waste of capacity, unless the mean field length is just a few positions.

This is, perhaps, the right place to note that the optimum coding theory pays no attention to how _complex_ the coding and decoding procedure and the associated hardware are. In practice, we have to compromise between the cost of the channel and the cost of the rest of the system. The flag bit is one such compromise.

3.5 Decipherable and Instant Codes

All the codes considered up to now have been such that code words have been assigned only to the ends of branches in the decision tree (with the exception of the end conditions of Table 4.).

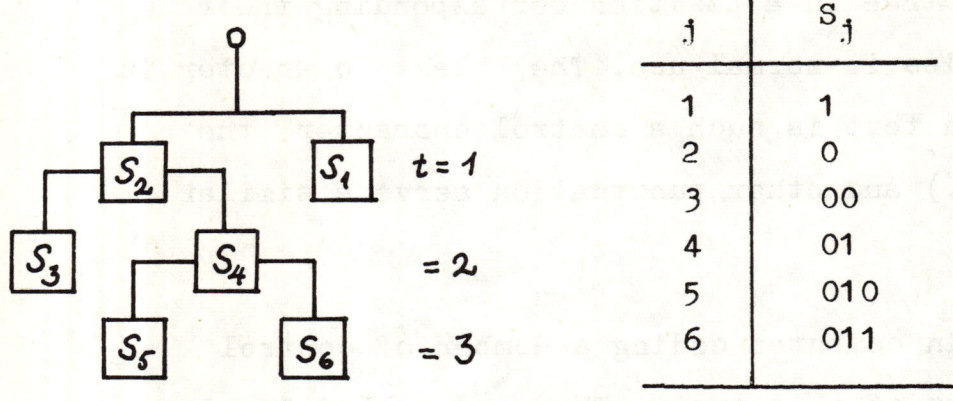

Fig. 7.

Table 5.

j	S_j
1	1
2	0
3	00
4	01
5	010
6	011

Consider the code of Fig. 7. and Table 5. If we have the following fragment of a message ...01100101001... there is more than one sequence of S_j that could generate this sequence, for example, $S_6 S_3 S_1 S_5 S_4$ or $S_4 S_1 S_3 S_1 S_4 S_3 S_1$. Taken separately every code word can be decoded uniquely by Table 5. But if no spaces or other separating symbols are to indicate the limits of the code words, the code cannot be interpreted uniquely.

A code is said to be <u>uniquely decipherable</u> if every finite sequence of code characters S_j corresponds to at most one message.

A sufficient condition (but not necessary) is that no code word is a "prefix" of another code word. The same condition means that the decision tree is not continued beyond any assigned code word.

The coding process of a uniquely decipherable code is reversible.

Consider, next, a code with the following two code words $S_1 = 0$, $S_2 = 01$. Character S_1 is a prefix of S_2. Is this code decipherable?

Let us look at a sample sequence

$$...0100100000101001...$$

It can be verified that only sequence

$$...\ S_2\ S_1\ S_2\ S_1\ S_1\ S_1\ S_2\ S_2\ S_1\ S_2\ ...$$

could generate it. It can be shown that this code is uniquely decipherable despite the fact that S_1 is a prefix of S_2. Notice that sequences with two or more successive 1's do not correspond to any sequence of S_1 and S_2.

This code has a special property that when ever we receive a zero (a prefix) we do not know the interpretation of it <u>before</u> receiving the next bit (the maximum number of bits followed by this prefix in a valid code word). A code with this property is called <u>non-instantaneous.</u>

A code is <u>instantaneous</u>, or an <u>instant code</u>, if the character S_j is uniquely determined after receiving its last bit (code element).

A uniquely decipherable code with no code word being a prefix of another is instantaneous.

Non-instantaneous codes are not normally used in data coding, but we find this property in the semantic information of natural languages. The same word can have different <u>meanings</u> in different contexts. The word that determines the context may come later in the sentence or in the next sentence, and the meaning is not uniquely determined before it.

A non-instantaneous decoding process requires <u>memory</u> where to store the segment of the message before it can be correctly interpreted.

CHAPTER 4

JOINT EVENTS, NATURAL LANGUAGES

4.1 Joint events

In previous chapters we have, so far, considered only messages in which successive characters and code words are statistically independent each occurring at a given probability p_j.

In real channels this is seldom the case. In this paragraph we shall first review some ststistical tools for the dependent case. These will be applied in subsequent paragraphs to develop the information rate of the conditional case and natural languages.

In order to have a specific case in mind, let us consider again the simplified English alphabet as defined on page 12.

The probabilities p_j as they appear in a standard English text are given in Table 6. arranged in the descending sequence by p_j. Table 7. gives the same statistics for German (L. Brillouin, L. Sacco).

char.	p_j	$-\log p_j$	char.	p_j	$-\log p_j$
space	.2	2.32	U	.0225	5.46
E	.105	3.25	M	.021	5.58
T	.072	3.79	P	.0175	5.81
O	.0654	3.93	Y	.012	6.35
A	.063	3.97	W	.012	6.35
N	.059	4.06	G	.011	6.49
I	.055	4.18	B	.0105	6.56
R	.054	4.20	V	.008	6.95
S	.052	4.26	K	.003	8.35
H	.047	4.40	X	.002	9.0
D	.035	4.84	J	.001	10.0
L	.029	5.10	Q	.001	10.0
C	.023	5.41	Z	.001	10.0
F	.0225	5.46			

Frequencies of letters in English text

Table 6.

char.	p_j	$-\log p_j$	char.	p_j	$-\log p_j$
space	.1442	2.80	O	.0211	5.57
E	.1440	2.80	M	.0172	5.84
N	.0865	3.53	B	.0138	6.18
S	.0646	3.95	W	.0113	6.45
I	.0628	3.99	Z	.0092	6.76
R	.0622	4.00	V	.0079	6.98
A	.0594	4.07	F	.0078	7.00
D	.0546	4.19	K	.0071	7.12
T	.0536	4.22	P	.0067	7.20
U	.0422	4.55	J	.0028	8.48
H	.0361	4.79	X	.0008	10.1
L	.0345	4.85	Q	.0005	11.0
C	.0255	5.28	Y	.0000	>14
G	.0236	5.41			

Frequencies of letters in German text (ö=oe, ä=ae, ü=ue)

Table 7.

Assuming still, for a moment, that the letters occur independently we may compute the information rates of English and German texts by the entropy (17). To indicate that we are using single letter frequencies we are giving a subscript 1.

English: $H_1 = 4.03$ bits/letter

German: $H_1 = 4.037$ bits/letter

For both languages the channel capacity, with constant $t_j = 1$, the channel capacity is

$$C = \log 27 = 4.76$$

In a natural language successive letters are not independent. For example, the probability of an "H" after a "T" in English is much higher than value .047 given in Table 6. Similarly hte probability of a "U" after a "Q" is almost 1.

Let us denote the joint probability of an ordered pair $S_i S_j$ of two letters by $p(i,j)$. These probabilities can be arranged in a two-dimensional array or matrix.

Notice, that matrix $p(i,j)$ is unsymmetric, $p(i,j) \neq p(j,i)$ since, for example, $p(H,T) < p(T,H)$.

The single letter frequencies are obtained from the matrix $p(i,j)$ as row or column sums.

$$(39) \quad p_i = \sum_{j=1}^{n} p(i,j) \quad ; \quad p_j = \sum_{i=1}^{n} p(i,j)$$

And, since

$$(40) \quad \sum_{i=1}^{n} p_i = \sum_{j=1}^{n} p_j = 1$$

the double summation

$$(41) \quad \sum_{i=1}^{n} \sum_{j=1}^{n} p(i,j) = \sum_{i,j} p(i,j) = 1$$

As in the Shannon-Fano method (see page 44) the ordered pairs $S_i S_j$ may be considered as a new set of n^2 characters with probabilities $p(i,j)$. Accordingly, if the statistical dependence does not extend further than to the next symbol, the information rate $I(i,j)$ of the n^2 symbols can be given by the entropy

$$(42) \quad I(i,j) = - \sum_{i,j} p(i,j) \log p(i,j)$$

The summation variables i and j do not, of course, appear as true variables in $I(i,j)$, which is a scalar quantity; they are included in the notation only to remind that $I(i,j)$ comes from the matrix $p(i,j)$.

In the same way $I(i)$ and $I(j)$ are going to be used to denote the information in p_i and p_j respectively.

$$(43) \quad \begin{aligned} I(i) &= -\sum_i p_i \log p_i = -\sum_{i,j} p(i,j) \log p_i \\ I(j) &= -\sum_j p_j \log p_j = -\sum_{i,j} p(i,j) \log p_j \end{aligned}$$

By adding the two equations (43)

$$(44) \quad I(i) + I(j) = -\sum_{i,j} p(i,j) \log p_i p_j$$

The summation in (44) is of same type as expression (22) with q_j replaced by $p_i p_j$. Thus, if

$$p_i p_j = p(i,j)$$

that is, the two symbols S_i and S_j are statistically independent, (44) is equal to (42). In all other cases by inequality (30) sum (44) is greater.

$$(45) \quad I(i) + I(j) \geq I(i,j)$$

The statistical dependence introduces an additional constraint to the system, and this has a decreasing effect on the information rate.

The same argument can be carried over to ordered groups of more than two symbols. If the statistical dependence extends over more than two consequtive symbols, as is the case in natural languages, the information rate is further reduced. This effect will be discussed further in Paragraph 4.3.

By applying (42) to the probabilities $p(i,j)$ of English and German (L. Sacco) it will be found that

$$\text{English:} \quad I(i,j) = 6.64$$
$$\text{German:} \quad I(i,j) = 6.80$$

This is the information rate per two letters. Let us denote by H_2 the entropy per letter from $p(i,j)$ (compare page 53) we have

$$\text{English:} \quad H_2 = 3.32 \text{ bits/letter}$$
$$\text{German:} \quad H_2 = 3.40 \text{ bits/letter}$$

which is a significant reduction from the single letter case H_1.

4.2. Conditional Information

In the preceding paragraph, when considering a pair $S_i S_j$ of symbols as a new character, we have assumed, implicitly, that the pair is received simultaneously, or no attention is paid to the stages of reception. This would be the case in a parallel reception.

Let us look at the reception of the same sequence of symbols in a serial mode, first S_i then S_j.

The serial mode is the more common mode of information transfer (telegraphy, radio transmission) due to considerably lower cost of equipment.

Visual perception is a case of parallel information transfer. A person looking at a picture is receiving simultaneously visual stimuli from every point of the picture through the complex system of the eye and optical nerves.

In television the transmission of the image is made serial by means of fast scanning of the picture. A parallel transmission of the same image with the same resolution would require about $600^2 = 360\ 000$ (number of lines $\cong 600$) low speed channels.

Let us take, as an illustration of the serial information transfer, a simple example of a census file.

The population is made up of 40% men and 60% women. Of all men (male) 30% are single, 50% married, 10% divorced and 10% widowed. Among the women the same percentages are 15, 45, 15, and 25.

The two pieces of information, sex and marital status, can be depicted by the decision tree of Fig. 8. by the two stages with 2 and 4 branches respectively.

We shall denote by p_i the probabilities of the first stage, p_1 for man and p_2 for woman. The probabilities at the second stage are dependent of the first choice i. The conditional probability of getting

- 58 -

one of the four possible answers to the second question, after knowing the sex, is denoted by $p_i(j)$. The four values $j = 1,2,3,4$ correspond to "single", "married", "divorced" and "widowed".

Table 8. gives the matrix $p_i(j)$ and array p_i.

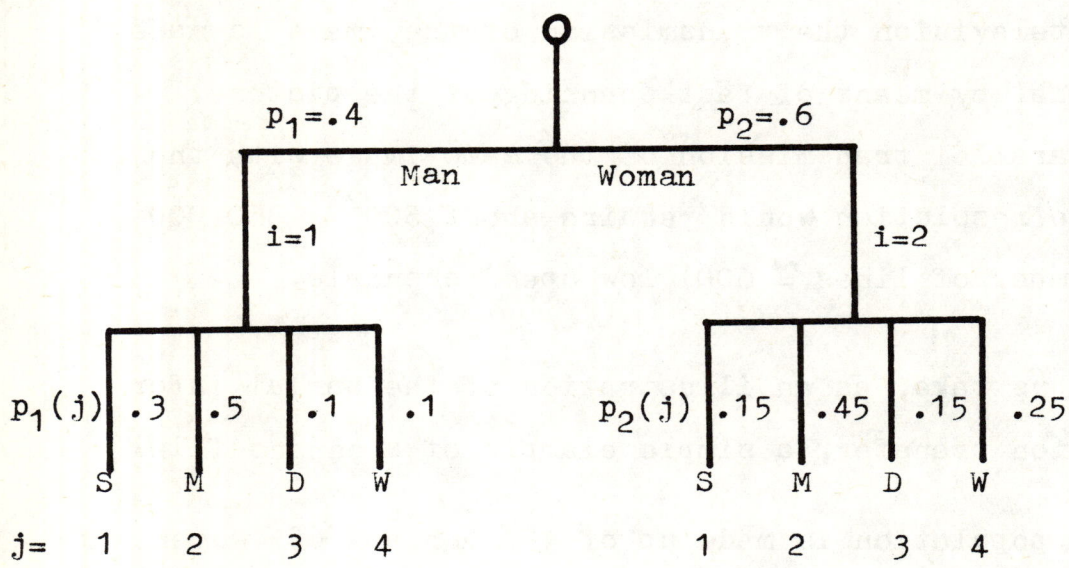

Fig. 8.

i \ j	sing. 1	marr. 2	div. 3	wid. 4		p_i
man 1	.3	.5	.1	.1		.4
wom. 2	.15	.45	.15	.25		.6

Table 8.
Matrix $p_i(j)$

The end points of the tree of Fig. 8. can be indicated by the pair of indices (i,j) and the probability of getting this pair of answers in the census poll is denoted in accordance with 4.2 by p(i,j).

This joint probability can be written as the product

(46) $\qquad p(i,j) = p_i \, p_i(j)$

of probabilities of first getting i and after that, on this condition, of getting j. Table 9. gives the numerical values of p(i,j) of the census example computed by (46) from Table 8.

i \ j	1	2	3	4	p_i
1	.12	.20	.04	.04	.4
2	.09	.27	.09	.15	.6
p_j	.21	.47	.13	.19	1

Table 9.

Matrix p(i,j)

We see by Equation (39) that the row and column sums of matrix (46) in Table 9. are p_i and p_j, respectively.

The same end information of the census poll could have been obtained by first asking the marital status and the sex after. This reversed decision tree is given in Fig. 9.

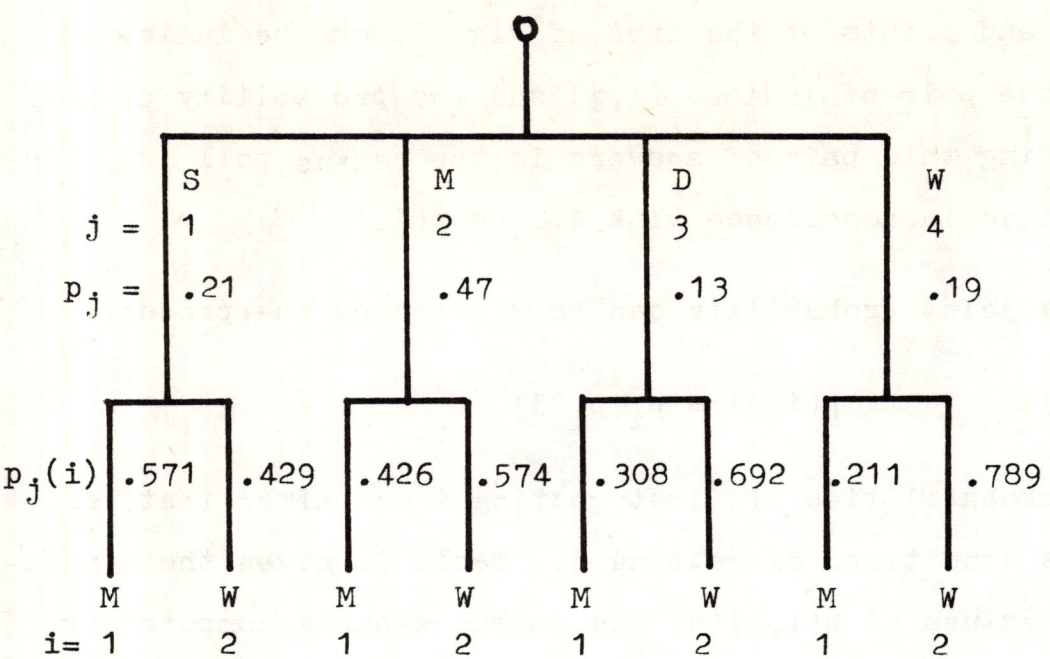

Fig. 9.

Evidently, we have for this case an equation of the same type as (46)

(47) $\quad p(i,j) = p_j \, p_j(i)$

where $p_j(i)$ is the conditional probability of i, given j.

The two conditional probabilities can be now written by using (46) and (47)

(48)
$$p_i(j) = \frac{p(i,j)}{p_i} = \frac{p_j}{p_i} p_j(i)$$
$$p_j(i) = \frac{p(i,j)}{p_j} = \frac{p_i}{p_j} p_i(j)$$

i \ j	1	2	3	4
1	.571	.426	.308	.211
2	.429	.574	.692	.789

Table 10.

Matrix $p_j(i)$

Let us denote again the information (entropy) in the unconditional distributions p_i and p_j by $I(i)$ and $I(j)$. By the same formalism, denote, further, the the information rates of distributions $p_i(j)$ and $p_j(i)$ by $I_i(j)$ and $I_j(i)$.

If, in Fig. 8., the first piece of information happens to be i = 1 (man) the second stage would have the mean information rate

$$I_1(j) = - \sum_{j=1}^{4} p_1(j) \log p_1(j) \;;(i = 1)$$

In the same way for the branch i = 2 (woman)

$$I_2(j) = - \sum_{j=1}^{4} p_2(j) \log p_2(j) \;;(i = 2)$$

To get the mean information rate of the second stage of the tree in Fig. 8. we add the two above cases weighted by their probabilities p_i

$$(49) \quad I_i(j) = \sum_i p_i \left[- \sum_j p_i(j) \log p_i(j) \right]$$

The same equation becomes by applying (46)

$$(50) \quad I_i(j) = - \sum_{i,j} p(i,j) \log p_i(j)$$

We can derive by the same approach the symmetrical equation

$$(51) \quad I_j(i) = - \sum_{i,j} p(i,j) \log p_j(i)$$

The mean information rate over the two stages is the sum $I(i) + I_i(j)$, which can be written by using equations (50), (43) and (44) as

$$\begin{aligned} I(i) + I_i(j) &= - \sum_{i,j} p(i,j) \log p_i \\ &\quad - \sum_{i,j} p(i,j) \log p_i(j) \\ (52) \quad &= - \sum_{i,j} p(i,j) \log(p_i p_i(j)) \\ &= - \sum_{i,j} p(i,j) \log p(i,j) = I(i,j) \end{aligned}$$

The end result of above development

$$(52) \quad I(i) + I_i(j) = I(i,j)$$

has a simple and self evident interpretation: Information received sequentially (in series) equals the same information received simultaneously (in parallel).

Inequality (45) and Equation (52) yield together

(53)
$$I(i) + I_i(j) = I(i,j) \leq I(i) + I(j)$$
$$I_i(j) \leq I(j)$$

(53) has the symmetrical counterpart

(54)
$$I(j) + I_j(i) = I(i,j) \leq I(i) + I(j)$$
$$I_j(i) \leq I(i)$$

The latter case corresponds to Fig. 9. that is, serial reception in the reversed order (receiving a message backwards).

Enequalities (53) and (54) indicate that the knowledge of the outcome of the first stage leaves less freedom of choice to the second stage than what was the original uncertainty (entropy). Hence, the information is also reduced.

In the census example we get the following numerical values

$$I(i) = .971, \quad I(j) = 1.823$$
$$I(i,j) = 2.749, \quad I_i(j) = 1.778, \quad I_j(i) = .926$$

4.3. Natural Languages

Natural languages are very complex information channels, even on the simplest, syntactic, level of information theory.

We have seen, already, in Paragraph 4.1 that the information rate of English (in the written form) is reduced from the channel capacity C = 4.76 bits/letter to H_1 = 4.03 bits/letter due to the letter frequencies given in Table 6. It was, also, found that the rate in a pair of letters, observing the statistical constraints $p(i,j)$, is still less, H_2 = 3.32 bits/letter.

This value, H_2, refers, however, only to an isolated pair $S_i S_j$ picked out of a text. What is the information rate per letter in a long message assuming that the probability $p_i(j)$ of the next letter S_j depends only on the preceding letter S_i, which has been already received?

In such a sequential reception the uncertainty (entropy) of the next letter is (except for the first letter of the message) always the conditional distribution $p_i(j)$. Consequently, the information rate is the conditional information $I_i(j)$.

In most text books of information theory $H_2 = \frac{1}{2} I(i,j)$ is given as the information rate for this case, but this implies that always every second letter (the first of the pair) has the uncertainty of p_i. Evidently this is not true for a long message.

We can compute $I_i(j)$ for English and German from the values of $I(i) = H_1$ and $I(i,j)$ on pages 53 and 56 by applying equation (52)

$$\text{English:} \quad I_i(j) = 6.64 - 4.03 = 2.61 \text{ bits/lett.}$$

$$\text{German:} \quad I_i(j) = 6.80 - 4.04 = 2.76 \text{ bits/lett.}$$

Is there a feasible coding scheme coding method based on $I_i(j)$, which would require only 2.61 bits of channel capacity per letter?

Yes. Assuming that we are given the probability matrix $p_i(j)$ we could design nearly optimum codes, according to the principles discussed in Paragraph 3.3, for each of the 27 rows of $p_i(j)$. That is, the first letter of a word would be coded by the optimum code based on the distribution $p_1(j)$ of letters S_j following the blank character (i = 1). If the first letter happens to be T (i = 3), the next letter is coded by picking up the code for the next letter from the optimum set of codes designed for distribution $p_3(j)$. The same scheme is applied to the rest of the message.

This coding system would be uniquely decipherable

and instantaneous. At reception the code key for the following letter is determined by the letter just received.

Assuming that each of the 27 individual codes can be made optimal, it can be readily shown that the capacity requirements (mean for a long message) is equal to $I_i(j)$ per letter. For an actual code the capacity would be slightly higher.

Again, no attention is given to the complexity of the "hardware" necessary for coding and decoding in the above system. But, if this is done by "software" in form of a table look-up program, and if efficient data compression is a prime requirement, the proposed coding scheme could be quite applicable.

In principle, the same approach could be carried further to triples of letters and so on indefinitely. What is the limiting information rate H_∞ of a very long message in English? Different estimation methods give a value which is between 1.5 and 2.0 bits per letter.

A further reduction to the actual information rate is introduced by semantic considerations. H_∞ is the syntactic limiting rate based on letter statistics. If the text is required also to be meaningful the additional constraints reduce the actual information rate to about 1 bit/letter.

In order to give an idea of the effect of increasing statistical constraints approximating a natural language, we have below four samples generated syntheticly by random numbers.

1) Picking up letters at random with equal probabilities $p_j = 1/27$

   LEXCCKM YGKKAHFAOJSVIMFDHLI PDZTCNLUHGHIKGWZIBUTAFKVFZB

2) Random selection of letters at probabilities p_j of Table 6.

   DSKATPRRY ATEKTEWINH WGNL NOAEIM R I HESBO SHSENK NNCE

3) Generating a string of letters by utilizing the conditional probabilities $p_i(j)$ for English.

   ESTOWHOPHEGG TONE OMAS INE INEXPUR OFANS TS T AT TYLIC

4) Picking whole words at random from an English text

   HAS COMMANDS KNELT MONEY IN COURSE HIGHER THE

Why is a natural language utilizing the channel so inefficiently? One reason is that a message of type 1) above is unpronounceable. In a spoken language the primary element is a syllable. If the orthography were based on syllables (hieroglyphs) the information rate would be much closer to the channel capacity.

There is, however, another reason why the information rate is so much less than the capacity. This property, called <u>redundancy</u>, makes a message intelligigible even at a certain error rate. A telegram message such as

CUMMING HOME TOWORROW APTERNOKN

can be still interpreted correctly in spite of the four errors.

A properly designed redundancy in a coding scheme is an efficient means of improving reliability (at the cost of information rate) in a noisy channel. These methods will be discussed in Chapter 5.

A measure R of the redundancy in a given code is defined in terms of the channel capacity $C = H_{max}$ and the information rate $I = H$ of the code.

$$(55) \quad R = \frac{H_{max} - H}{H_{max}} = 1 - H/H_{max}$$

R is a dimensionless number $0 \leq R \leq 1$.

Notice the difference between the coding efficiency (21) and the redundancy (55). The former is a relationship between information rate and capacity used by code, the latter between information rate and channel capacity.

k	H_k	R_k	k	H_k	R_k
1	4.03	.15	1	4.04	.15
2	3.32	.30	2	3.40	.29
3	3.10	.35	3	2.80	.41
∞	1.70	.64	∞	1.60	.66
English			German		

Table 11.

Table 11. summarizes the information rates H_k for multiple letter groups in English and German and the redundancies computed by (55) assuming $H_{max}= 4.76$.

Let us consider, next, a natural language as a coding system, in which the words are viewed as the basic elements, that is, a variable length character set S_j with lengths t_j and probabilities p_j. If the words ocurred statistically independently (which they do not) the optimum language, from the point of view of information rate, should have word lengths in accordance with Equation (36). The more frequent a word is the shorter it should be.

Table 12. gives the most frequent words in English telegram text and their probabilities. We observe that they all are short, monosyllable words. In other types of text such as conversational language we would find somewhat different ranking of words. Word "I" missing in Table 12. would occupy a relatively high position (rank). In a telegraph text it is often omitted since it can be implied from context (see example on page 68).

j	S_j	p_j	$-\log_k p_j$	j	S_j	p_j	$-\log_k p_j$
1	THE	.08	.77	8	IT	.01	1.40
2	TO	.03	1.06	9	FOR	.01	1.40
3	OF	.03	1.06	10	HAS	.01	1.40
4	A	.02	1.19	11	ON	.01	1.40
5	IN	.02	1.19	12	OR	.01	1.40
6	AND	.02	1.19	13	AT	.01	1.40
7	IS	.02	1.19				

(k = 27)

Table 12.

It is seen immediately that the word lengths (t_j = number of letters + space) are much too long for an optimum code. This is to be expected due to the redundancy.

An interesting observation in Table 12. is that the 13 most frquent words account for about 28% of all words in telegraph messages.

If the list of words arranged in a sequence of decreasing frequencies p_j is extended beyond that of Table 12. it is found that there is an approximate relationship between the rank j and probability p_j known as the Zipf's Law

(56) $$p_j \cong A/j$$

where A is a constant. For English $A \cong 0.1$.

Notice, also, that a written natural language is an instantaneous code since, as soon as we receive a blank character, we know that it is the end of the word S_j. Hence, the vocabulary can be represented by a k-nary (k = 27) decision tree with S_j's only at the terminations of branches. A high proportion of the terminations are unused, that is, all the possible words not in the vocabulary of the language.

By substituting (56) in the entropy expression (17) we get the information rate per word in English

$$I_w = 11.82 \text{ bits/word}$$

Further, it is found that the mean word length in English is 4.5 letters plus the word space or total of 5.5 printing positions. Thus, the mean information rate is on the word level

$$I_w = 11.82/5.5 = 2.14 \text{ bits/letter}$$

Now, this information rate is obtained by assuming independence between successive words. The additional constraints of grammar between words in a sentence bring this rate down to about 1.7 bits/letter (Table 11.). And, finally, the semantic constraints (sentences that make sense) reduce it to about 1 bit/letter.

CHAPTER 5

NOISY CHANNEL

5.1 Channel Matrix and Information Rate

In the previous chapters we have assumed that the message is always received without a possibility of error. So, for example, in a binary channel a received "1" implies with certainty a transmitted "1".

In this chapter we are going to discuss the opposite case where an error is possible with a certain non-zero probability. This effect, resulting in an uncertainty of the transmitted information, is called noise.

Let us consider, as an introductory example, a binary channel $S_1 = 0$, $S_2 = 1$, $p_1 = 3/4$, $p_2 = 1/4$. with a 10% error rate. That means, 10% of S_1's are received as S_2 and 10% of S_2's are received as S_1. We assume, further, that successive S_j and errors occur statistically independently.

The transmitted information I is defined as the difference in entropy (uncertainty) before (à priori) and after (à posteriori) reception.

Since the à posteriori probabilities are conditional on the received character, we have to apply concepts introduced in Paragraph 4.2.

The error condition, as given in the problem definition on the preceding page, is expressed by the conditional probability $p_i(j)$ of receiving character S_j on condition that S_i was transmitted. This matrix, given for the example case in Table 13., defines uniquelly the error (noise) properties of the channel. It is called the channel matrix. The same matrix is called by many authors also the likelihood matrix.

i \ j	1	2	p_i
1	.9	.1	.75
2	.1	.9	.25

Table 13.
Matrix $p_i(j)$
Vector p_i

In the following discussion the index i refers always to the transmitted symbol and j to the received symbol.

Thus, p_i is the à priori distribution of probabilities of transmitted symbols S_i. ($p_1 = .75$, $p_2 = .25$ for p_i)

The probability $p(i,j)$ of the joint event of transmitting an S_i and receiving an S_j is by (46)

(57) $$p(i,j) = p_i\, p_i(j)$$

and by (39) the distribution p_j of received symbols S_j is

(58) $$p_j = \sum_{i=1}^{n} p(i,j)$$

that is, the column sums of matrix (57). Matrix (57) and vector (58) are given for the binary example in Table 14.

i \ j	1	2
1	.675	.075
2	.025	.225
p_j	.70	.30

Table 14.
Matrix $p(i,j)$
Vector p_j

It is interesting to note that the distribution p_j of S_j at the receiving end is different from p_i inspite of the symmetric error properties as given by the channel matrix of Table 13.

The **à posteriori probability** of a transmitted symbol S_i **after** the reception of S_j, is the conditional probability $p_j(i)$ as given by (47) and (48)

(59) $$p_j(i) = \frac{p(i,j)}{p_j} = \frac{p_i}{p_j} p_i(j)$$

For the numerical values of $p_j(i)$ in the example see Table 15.

The process of transmission over a noisy channel can be visualized by the schematic diagram of Fig. 10.

i \ j	1	2
1	.964	.250
2	.036	.750

Table 15.

Matrix $p_j(i)$

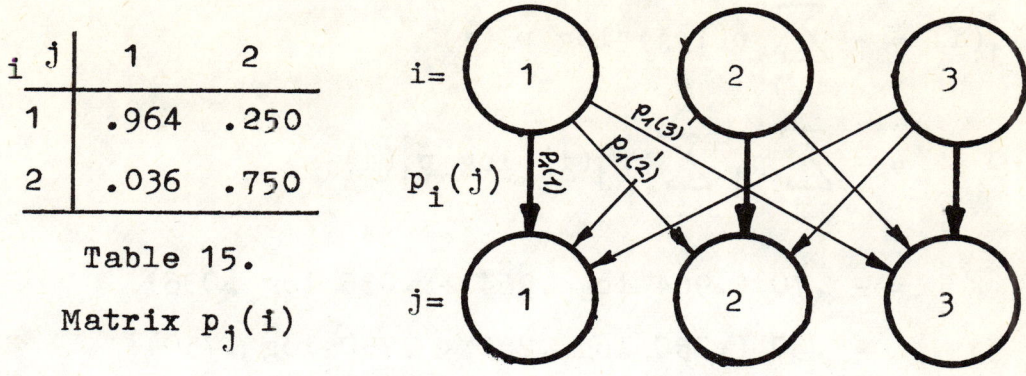

Fig. 10.

By applying the definition of information rate in the noisy channel as given on the top of page 73, we notice that the à priori entropy is by the denotation of Paragraph 4.2 the entropy of p_i or $I(i)$. The à posteriori entropy is by the same argument the entropy of $p_j(i)$. Thus, the information rate I is

$$(60) \qquad I = I(i) - I_j(i)$$

By applying the equality

$$(61) \qquad I(i) + I_i(j) = I(j) + I_j(i) = I(i,j)$$

we get the symmetric expression for I

$$(62) \qquad I = I(j) - I_i(j)$$

For our example

$$I(i) = \frac{3}{4} \log(4/3) + \frac{1}{4} \log(4/1) = .811$$

$$I_j(i) = -\sum_{i,j} p(i,j) \log p_j(i)$$

$$= -\sum_j p_j \sum_i p_j(i) \log p_j(i)$$

$$= -.70 \,(.964 \log .964 + .036 \log .036)$$
$$ -.30 \,(.250 \log .250 + .750 \log .750)$$

$$= .400$$

And
$$I = .811 - .400 = .411 \quad \text{bits/character}$$

The same numerical outcome is obtained by using (62). It is left to the reader to verify this. It is seen that, due to the noise, only half of the original information is received.

As $I_j(i)$ cannot be negative, the maximum information rate (60) is equal to $I(i)$ when $I_j(i) = 0$. This means, that there is no à posteriori uncertainty. The minimum I is obtained in case $p(i,j) = p_i p_j$, or the received and transmitted characters are statistically independent. In this case $p_j(i) = p_i$ by (48) and

$$I_j(i) = -\sum_{i,j} p_i p_j \log p_i = -\sum_i p_i \log p_i = I(i)$$

The à posteriori entropy is equal to à priori entropy and no information is transmitted. $I = 0$.

(63) $\qquad 0 \leq I \leq I(i)$

5.2 Capacity of Noisy Channel

We have derived in the preceding paragraph the information rate for a channel whose channel matrix and à priori probabilities p_i are given. In paragraph 2.3 we defined the information content (rate) in terms of the minimum capacity that can carry the information. Now, we use the same approach in reverse by defining the capacity of the noisy channel as the maximum rate of information that can be transferred by the channel.

Let us assume that the channel matrix $p_i(j)$ and the associated character set S_i are fixed. We are trying to find the à priori distribution p_i that maximizes the information rate I. This rate I_{max} is at the same time the capacity of the channel.

We shall use, for this purpose, equation (62) and investigate first the second term $I_i(j)$.

$$(64) \quad I_i(j) = - \sum_{i,j} p(i,j) \log p_i(j)$$

$$= - \sum_i p_i \sum_j p_i(j) \log p_i(j)$$

The general case of an arbitrary channel matrix leads to analytic difficulties. Therefore, we are going to limit ourselves in this discussion to a special case called a <u>symmetric channel</u>.

A channel is called symmetric if the channel matrix $p_i(j)$ has the following properties. Each row contains the same set of numbers. The columns have the same property, but the two sets are not necessarily the same for rows and columns, except when the matrix is a square matrix.

The channel matrix of Table 13. is symmetric. The set of numbers for rows and columns is .9 and .1.

Due to the defining property, the entropies of all rows of $p_i(j)$ are equal, say, H_r. This simplifies (64) to

$$(65) \qquad I_i(j) = \sum_i p_i(H_r) = H_r$$

Since, now, (65) is independent of p_i the maximum rate I_{max} is obtained by maximizing

$$I(j) = -\sum_j p_j \log p_j$$

which implies that p_j is the uniform distribution $p_j = 1/n$. But

$$(66) \qquad p_j = \sum_i p(i,j) = \sum_i p_i\, p_i(j) = 1/n$$

In a symmetric matrix, by definition, all columns of $p_i(j)$ have the same numbers in different permutations. Under these conditions (66) is possible if, and only if, also $p_i = 1/n$ for all i.

Thus, in a symmetric matrix, the maximum information rate, equal to the channel capacity, is obtained by a uniform à priori distribution $p_i = 1/n$. The capacity C is

(67) $\qquad C = \log n - H_r$

where H_r is the entropy of a (any) row of the channel matrix.

By comparing (67) with the noiseless capacity (5) we see that the noise reduces the capacity by the amount H_r.

In the example of Paragraph 5.1 the channel capacity becomes

$$C = \log 2 - (-0.9 \log 0.9 - 0.1 \log 0.1)$$
$$= .531 \text{ bits/character}$$

Compare this with the information rate $I = .411$ on page 76.

For the <u>unsymmetric channel</u> we are going to take only a simple numerical case.

Assume that the two states of a binary channel are $S_1 = 0 =$ no current, $S_2 = 1 =$ current in the communication circuit. Suppose that the power supply is running low, and therefore detection of the current at the receiver is uncertain. The "no current" is always received correctly. The channel matrix of Table 16. indicates that only 3/4 of the current pulses are detected. The matrix is unsymmetrical.

i \ j	1	2	p_i
1	1	0	1-p
2	1/4	3/4	p

Table 16.
Matrix $p_i(j)$
Vector p_i

i \ j	1	2
1	1-p	0
2	p/4	3p/4
p_j	$\frac{4-3p}{4}$	$\frac{3p}{4}$

Table 17.
Matrix $p(i,j)$
Vector p_j

The à priori probabilities p_i are denoted (1-p) and p where p is for the moment indeterminate. Our problem is to find p that maximizes the information rate (62).

Table 17. contains $p(i,j)$ and p_j computed from the data of Table 16. by equations (57) and (58). We substitute p_j of Table 17. to the second of equations (43) and multiply by 4.

$$4I(j) = (4-3p) \log\left(\frac{4}{4-3p}\right) + 3p \log(4/3p)$$

From Table 16. the conditional information $I_i(j)$ becomes

$$I_i(j) = -(1-p)\left[1 \log 1 + 0 \log 0\right]$$
$$- p\left[\frac{1}{4}\log(1/4) + \frac{3}{4}\log(3/4)\right]$$

We notice that the first term (entropy of the first row) is zero. We substitute these two expressions in (62) multiplied by 4.

$$4I = 4(I(j) - I_i(j))$$
$$= 8(1-p) - (4-3p)\log(4-3p) - 3p \log p$$

We set the derivative of I equal to zero

$$4(dI/dp) = -8 + 3 \log \frac{4-3p}{p} = 0$$

which has the approximate solution

$$p = .43 = p_i, \quad i = 2$$
$$1-p = .57 = p_i, \quad i = 1$$

By p_j in Table 17.

$$j = 1, \quad p_j = .677$$
$$j = 2, \quad p_j = .323$$

Further

$$I(j) = .908$$
$$I_i(j) = .350$$

and the maximum information rate, that is, channel capacity, is

$$I_{max} = C = .908 - .350 = .558 \text{ bits/character}$$

5.3 Ideal Observer

Consider a case of information transmission where at the transmitting end the character set S_i has fewer characters than the set S_j at the receiving end. This would be the case when all possible code words of the decision tree were not assigned a symbol (invalid code words). For example, in the garbled telegraph message on page 68 only one word, HOME, is a valid English "code word". If we assume that only proper English words will be transmitted but also erroneous words can be received, we have the set S_j greater than S_i. See also Paragraph 5.4 on error checking and correcting codes.

i \ j	1	2	3	p_i
1	3/4	0	1/4	4/5
2	0	3/4	1/4	1/5

Table 18. Matrix $p_i(j)$

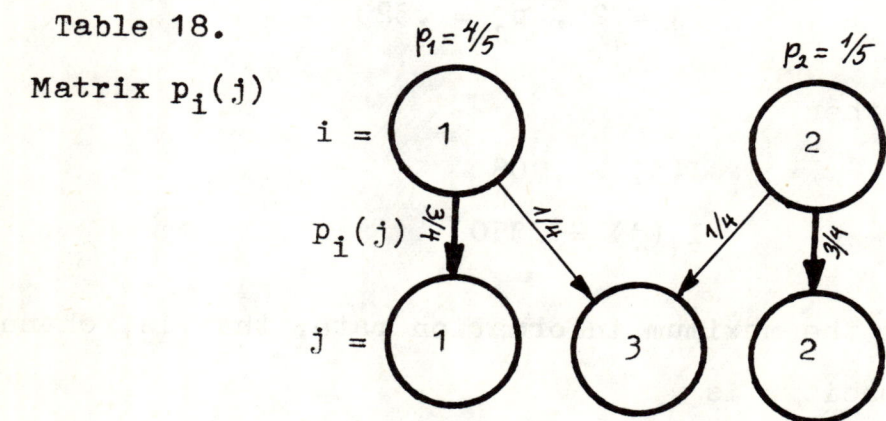

Fig. 11.

Table 18. gives the channel matrix of a simple case with a binary set S_i and ternary set S_j. The same channel is illustrated in Fig. 11. Symbols $S_{i=1}$ and $S_{i=2}$ are transmitted with à priori probabilities $p_{i=1} = 4/5$ and $p_{i=2} = 1/5$. 1/4 of both S_i are incorrectly received as the invalid $S_{j=3}$ symbol or code word.

The mean information rate from i to j denoted I_{ij} can be computed as in 5.1. (Notice that $p_i(j)$ is not a square matrix, and the channel is unsymmetric since the columns do not have the same set of numbers.)

$$I_{ij} = I(i) - I_j(i)$$

$$= .722 - .181 = .541 \text{ bits/symbol}$$

What is the best procedure when the invalid symbol $S_{j=3}$ is received?

This event implies a transmission error, and a plausible action would be to request retransmission. Let us assume, however, that this is not possible. This is often the case in real-time data processing systems, where we have no possibility of reenacting the event generating the erroneous data. We are in the same situation as receiving a garbled telegraph message from a party whose address is unknown.

In a teleprocessing system with data transmission from punched cards or tape the retransmission is possible when the error is detected immediately during transmission. The same applies to data transfer between, say, magnetic tape units and the central processing unit (CPU) of a computer system.

At present, then, our problem consists in defining an interpretation to the symbol $S_{j=3}$ that would preserve as much as possible of the source information $I(i) = .722$ bits/symbol.

Our first approach is the following: Since 4/5 of the invalid symbols are generated by $S_{i=1}$ and 1/5 by $S_{i=2}$ we are going to use the "best guess" by iterpreting $S_{j=3}$ as S_1 or S_2 at random in the same ratio 4 to 1. We denote the outcome of this process S_k (k = 1,2). This reception scheme and the channel matrix $p_j(k)$ are given in Fig. 12. and Table 19.

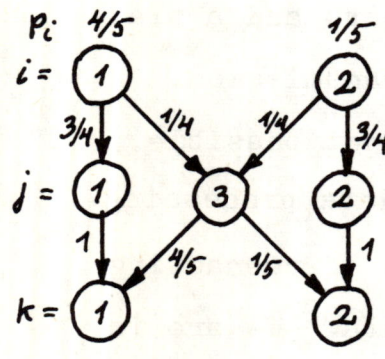

Fig. 12.

j \ k	1	2	p_j
1	1	0	12/20
2	0	1	3/20
3	4/5	1/5	5/20

Table 19.

Matrix $p_j(k)$

The probabilities p_j in Table 19. are obtained from Table 18. as

$$p_j = \sum_i p(i,j) = \sum_i p_i\, p_i(j)$$

The channel matrix $p_i(k)$ from the source to the final, interpreted form is apparently the product matrix of $p_i(j)$ and $p_j(k)$.

(68) $$p_i(k) = \sum_j p_i(j)\, p_j(k)$$

This matrix is given in Table 20. and the inverse conditional probability $p_k(i)$ in Table 21.

i \ k	1	2	p_i
1	19/20	1/20	4/5
2	1/5	4/5	1/5

Table 20.

Matrix $p_i(k)$

i \ k	1	2	p_i
1	19/20	1/5	4/5
2	1/20	4/5	1/5

Table 21.

Matrix $p_k(i)$

From matrix $p_k(i)$ of Table 21. we get

$$I_k(i) = .372$$

and the information rate I_{ik} from i to k

$$I_{ik} = I(i) - I_k(i) = .722 - .372 = .350$$

By comparing I_{ik} with I_{ij} on page 83, it is seen that .191 bits of information are lost in the process of interpretation according to the scheme of Fig. 12.

We can generalize equation (68) for a channel that can be broken down to successive stages in tandem such as from i to j and j to k. The channel matrix for the composite channel is the product of the channel matrices of the individual sections of the channel.

Is the above scheme of interpretation the best possible?

We try, next, a deterministic interpretation method. Since it is more probable that $S_{j=3}$ was generated by $S_{i=1}$ than $S_{i=2}$ we interpret $S_{j=3}$ <u>always</u> as S_1. Matrices $p_j(k)$ and $p_k(i)$ for this case are given in Tables 22. and 23.

j \ k	1	2
1	1	0
2	0	1
3	1	0

Table 22.
matrix $p_j(k)$

i \ k	1	2
1	16/17	0
2	1/17	1

Table 23.
Matrix $p_k(i)$

The information rate I_{ik} is computed as before

$$I_{ik} = I(i) - I_k(i) = .722 - .218 = .504$$

and we see that this deterministic scheme retains more of the information than the first based on "guess work".

It can be shown that in a general case the scheme of interpretation that assigns an invalid code word the most probable valid code word assures the highest information rate. This process is called the <u>ideal observer</u>.

If for some invalid code word there is more than one valid word the system is degenerate. But even in this case a deterministic scheme with any of the equal interpretations chosen gives the maximum rate of transferred information.

In the above case the rate $I_{ik} = .504$ of the ideal observer is less than $I_{ij} = .541$. That is, even the ideal observer destroys a part of the information that was initially received. At the stage k we no longer know if there was a transmission error or not. This is exactly the information that is lost by the observer.

CHAPTER 6

ERROR CHECKING AND CORRECTING CODES

6.1 Hamming Distance, Parity Checking

In this chapter we are going to discuss properties of a channel of the same type as in 5.3, that is, a channel with the character set S_j having more characters than S_i. The characters in excess are known, when received, to be invalid and indicate an error of transmission. In this chapter we assume that we have recourse to the source data when an error has been detected.

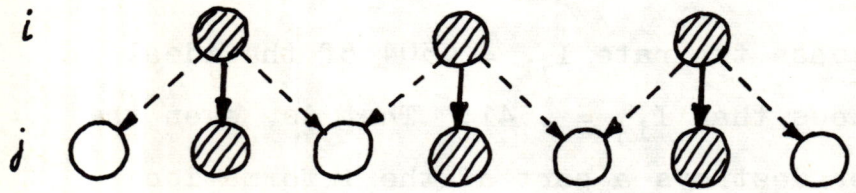

Fig. 13.

Fig. 13. illustrates the principle of such an error checking code. The shaded circles represent valid and the open circles invalid code words.

The heavy arrows represent an error free reception with probability $p_i(j)$ almost unity ($i=j$), the dotted arrows ($i \neq j$) are transmission errors. It is assumed in the schematics of Fig. 13. that the probability of an error generating another valid S_j is negligible (no arrows).

How should we design a coding system with the error checking properties of Fig. 13 ?

This depends, evidently, on the mechanism or statistical behavior of the error generation. The simplest assumption (assuming binary code) is that bit errors occur independently with a constant (low) probability, say, p.

Under these conditions the probability of having s bit errors in a string of m bits is distributed binomially.

(69) $\qquad P(s) = \binom{m}{s} p^s (1-p)^{m-s} \; ; \quad 0 \leq s \leq m$

From this expression we have in particular

(70)
$\qquad P(0) = (1-p)^m \qquad \text{no error}$
$\qquad P(1) = m\, p(1-p)^{m-1} \qquad \text{single error}$
$\qquad P(2) = \tfrac{1}{2} m(m-1)\, p^2 (1-p)^{m-2}$
$\qquad \qquad \qquad \qquad \qquad \text{double error}$

Given $p \ll 1$ we can find an m such that the probability of a multiple error ($s > 1$) is less than a specified small risk probability e of an undetected error.

For example, assuming p = .01 and e = .001 we would have m ≤ 5.

Let us define a distance d_{ij}, the so called <u>Hamming distance</u>, between two (binary) code words of equal length as the number of bit positions that are unequal. For example, the two code words S_i = 1001 and S_j = 0101 differ in the first two bit positions and have a distance d_{ij} = 2.

The Hamming distance is, at the same time, the minimum number of bit errors that can change the transmitted S_i into a received S_j.

Using fixed length (m bits) binary code words and assuming the probability e of multiple bit errors in a code word negligible, a sufficient and necessary condition for an error checking code is that the valid code words are at a minimum Hamming distance of 2 from one another. Such a code is called an error checking code of the first order the order being the level of multiple errors detected.

A binary code word of m bits can be conceived as a vector (point) in an m-dimensional space each bit position representing an orthogonal axis. We call this space the <u>code space</u>. Figure 14. illustrates the binary code space for m = 3. If the shaded circles are selected to be the valid and the open circles the invalid code words we can verify that the minimum distance of any two valid code words is $d_{ij} = 2$.

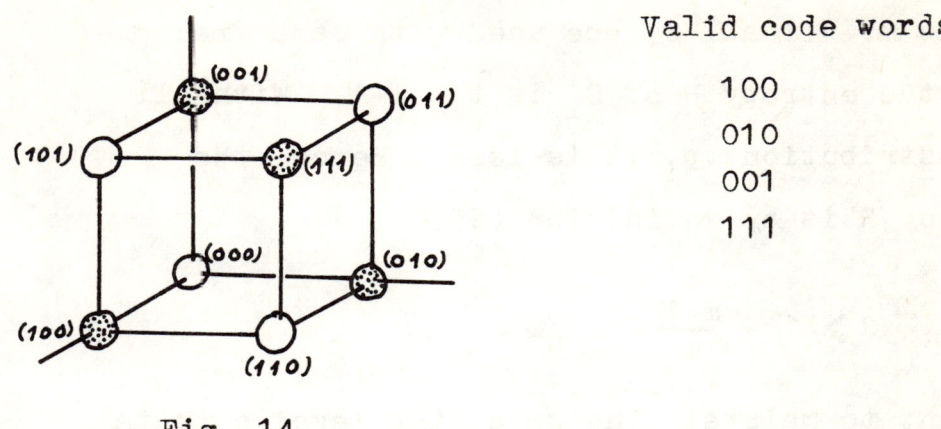

Valid code words
100
010
001
111

Fig. 14.

If we take the complementary set as the valid code words (interchanging valid and invalid sets) this code has the same property.

A valid code word in Fig. 14. is recognized by the property that it has an odd number of bits = 1, a code with an odd <u>parity check</u>. The complementary set has an even parity check.

In this code we can identify the check bit as, say, the last and say that the parity check code of length m has m-1 = t information bits and one check bit. The number of valid code words $n = 2^t = 2^{m-1}$.

Notice in Fig. 14. that the Hamming distance d_{ij} is the number of edges of the "cube" from S_i to S_j.

What is the maximum information rate and the redundancy of a parity error checking code?

The maximum entropy H_{max} of a binary code word of m bits is m. If all S_i are used with same frequensies p_i the entropy H of S_i is t = m-1. With all other distributions p_i it is less. Hence, the redundancy R is by definition (55)

(71) $\quad R \geq 1 - \frac{m-1}{m} = 1/m$

If we want to maintain the same risk level e (rate of undetected errors) with an increasing error probability p it will be seen by the argument at the bottom of page 89 that m has to be decreased, that is, we have to increase the redundancy of the code with increasing noise level in order to maintain same reliability. (See also page 68)

Redundancy as such is, however, no guarantee of reliability. It has to be carefully designed based on the properties of the noise.

All error checking codes are, by necessity, redundant (R > 0). Therefore, these methods are also called redundancy checking.

We can build into an information system a hierarchy of redundancy checks. Consider an m-bit parity checking code. Divide a long message of M characters into blocks of m_w characters. Call these blocks message words. These message words may be now considered as constituting a new character set S_i', and we can apply redundancy check on the level of the message words. When properly designed, this method would improve the reliability through the detection of most multiple bit errors that escaped detection on the level of S_i.

The same method could be carried further to blocks of message words in a hierarchy of redundancy checks. Detection of an error on a certain level requires a repetition of the entire block in question.

This method is used, for example, in data transfer between tape units and the CPU. An additional check character LRC (longitudinal redundancy check) is generated automatically at the end of each data record such that each track of the tape record gets the right bit parity.

Same method is used also in inventory codes. If the code consists of, say, 5 numerical digits an additional digit is added to the end of the code such that the digits add up to an easily checkable number, for example, a multiple of ten. This is done to detect punching errors or erroneously entered code at a real time terminal.

Parity chacking is also used universally in computers to check operations and data transfer internal to the CPU.

A commonly used form of redundancy checking in human communication is repetition. The whole "message" is retransmitted. An error free transmission is implied by a matching repetition. In this case we have minimum redundancy R = ½.

En error checking system can never be 100% reliable. How efficient and highly redundant we ever make the checking system there always remains a non-zero probability of an undetected error. But it is always possible to design a system with an arbitrary small risk level e > 0.

(For example, a certain number of typing errors are unavoidable in a book of this size in spite of repeated proofreadings.)

6.2 Error Corecting Codes, Hamming Bound

Consider the redundancy code of Fig. 15. with a minimum distance d_{ij} = 3 between any two valid code words. This code, having a higher redundancy than that of Fig. 13., could be used for detecting errors up to the second order (two bit errors in word of m bits).

Note that the parity checking code (Fig. 14.) detects all odd order errors.

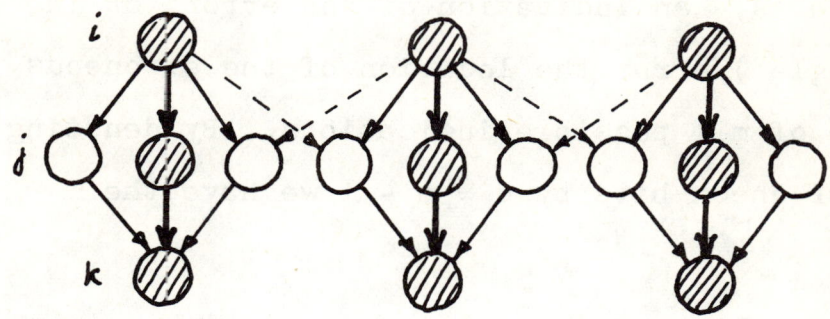

Fig. 15.

The reception of this code could be, as well, based on the principle of the ideal observer.

Let us assume, as in the case of independent bit errors, that the conditional probability $p_i(j)$ (channel matrix) is decreasing monotonically with the Hamming distance d_{ij}. An alternate way would be to define a generalized code distance D_{ij} by means of a suitable monotonic function of $p_i(j)$.

The lowest row of circles in Fig. 15. indicates the operation of the ideal observer. It is seen that errors of the first order are <u>corrected</u> and errors of higher orders (multiple bit errors) cause an incorrect interpretation. This is a first order <u>error correcting code</u>.

If we limit ouselves, again, to fixed length code words of m bits, what are the requirements for such an error correcting code?

Each code word has to carry, in addition to the t information bits, an indication of "no error" or in case of (single) error the location of the erroneous bit, a total of m+1 possible indications. By denoting the number of check bits by $c = m - t$ we have the condition

(72) $\qquad 2^c \geq m + 1$

Table 24. gives a few cases of (72) for which the equality is satisfied

c	m	t
1	1	0
2	3	1
3	7	4
4	15	11
5	31	26
6	63	57

Table 24.

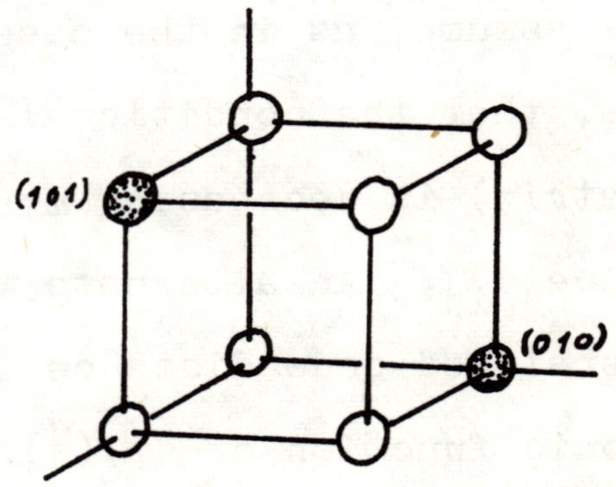

Fig. 16.

Fig. 16. illustrates the case $c = 2$, $m = 3$. This binary first order error correcting code requires 2 check bits for one information bit and has the minimum redundancy $R = 2/3$.

If the number of information bits required for the character set is not one those listed in Table 24. the number c of check bits is that of the next higher in the same table. For example, to have a character set of 64 symbols, $t = 6$ and $c = 4$ giving a code word length $m = 10$.

It is seen from Table 24. that by using longer code words we can get a correcting code with a lower redundancy. But this, assuming a fixed risk level e, implies a lower bit error rate p.

We know that a higher redundancy means a lower rate of information through the channel. On the other hand, a higher noise level (p) gives a lower channel capacity. These two facts, we have seen repeatedly, seem to be interrelated.

This relationship, which we are not going to prove, is known as the Fundamental Theorem of Information Theory:

It is possible to transmit information through a noisy channel with an arbitrarily small probability of error if, and only if, the rate of information is less than the channel capacity.

The theorem does not tell how to achieve such a coding system but it tells, what is often as important, what is impossible to achieve.

	S_i		S_i
i	ABCD EFG	i	ABCD EFG
1	0000 111	9	1000 000
2	0001 100	10	1001 011
3	0010 010	11	1010 101
4	0011 001	12	1011 110
5	0100 001	13	1100 110
6	0101 010	14	1101 101
7	0110 100	15	1110 011
8	0111 111	16	1111 000

Table 25.

Another example of the first order error correcting codes is given in Table 25. This corresponds to the third line of Table 24. with $t = 4$, $c = 3$, $m = 7$. It is left to the reader to verify that all distances d_{ij} are at least 3.

The method of error correction in the code of Table 25. is based on the parity of the three sums

$$
\begin{aligned}
A + B + C + E &= P_1 \\
A + B + D + F &= P_2 \\
A + C + D + G &= P_3
\end{aligned}
\tag{73}
$$

where the letters A to D are the values of the information bits and E to G those of the three check bits.

If all P_i have an odd parity there is no error. The remaining 7 parity combinations indicate the location of the (single) error according to Table 26.

error location	parity P₁	P₂	P₃
A	+	+	+
B	+	+	−
C	+	−	+
D	−	+	+
E	+	−	−
F	−	+	−
G	−	−	+

\+ = even
− = odd

Table 26.

If the check bits EFG in Table 25. are replaced by their complements we have another code operating on reversed parity of P_i.

Other codes utilizing longer code words can be based on similar parity checks. The hardware required for these operations consists of fairly simple logical circuits.

We can now easily generalize the error checking and correcting code requirements based on the Hamming distance. We have seen that the minimum distance $d_{ij} = 2$ makes a first order checking code possible. Minimum distance $d_{ij} = 3$ can generate a second order checking or first order correcting code. Similarly, a minimum distance $d_{ij} = 4$ can be used for a third order checking or for a first order correcting <u>and</u>

second order checking code.

In general, for an error correcting code of order r the minimum distance is $d_{ij} = 2r + 1$. We can think of each valid code word to be surrounded by a "sphere of influence" of radius $r + \frac{1}{2}$. If these spheres in the code space do not overlap we have secured the minimum distances.

The number of code word (points) inside this sphere (one valid and the rest invalid) is

$$(74) \qquad \sum_{d=0}^{r} \binom{m}{d} = N(r)$$

where d is a distance and $\binom{m}{d}$ is the number of combination of code words at this distance from the valid code word.

The number af all possible code words (size of the code space) is 2^m. If a code with a character set of n symbols is required the total "volume" of n spheres (74) may not exceed 2^m. Hence

$$(75) \qquad n \sum_{d=0}^{r} \binom{m}{d} \leq 2^m$$

This limiting inequality is called the Hamming Bound.

For the case $n = 2^t$, $r = 1$ and $c = m-t$ (75) reduces to inequality (72).

6.3 Some Other Redundancy Codes

In the preceding two paragraph an underlying assumption has been that individual bit errors occur independently. In real information channels this is seldom the case. For example, in data transmission over a communication circuit, an external disturbance causing a bit error may often last longer than one bit time. Consequently, errors tend to appear in bursts.

One type of redundancy code that seems to be more reliable against bursts of errors than the parity codes of same redundancy is the k-out-of-m code.

In such a code each valid code word of length m has exactly k (k<m) bit positions equal to 1 and m-k positions equal to 0. The number n of valid code words is

$$(76) \qquad n = \binom{m}{k} = \frac{m!}{k!\,(m-k)!}$$

and the minimum redundancy

$$(77) \qquad R = 1 - \frac{\log n}{m}$$

In the 2-out-of-5 code we have $n = \binom{5}{2} = 10$, which is just enough for coding of decimal information. Table 27. gives a possible allocation of this code.

digit	code	digit	code
0	00011	5	01100
1	00101	6	10001
2	00110	7	10010
3	01001	8	10100
4	01010	9	11000

Table 27.

If all digits (S_i) occur at equal probabilities $p_i = .1$ and independently, the information rate is $I = \log n = \log 10 = 3.322$. The redundancy is $R = 1 - 3.322/5 = .3356$.

In a k-out-of-m code we cannot identify the information bits and check bits as in the parity codes. So, for example, above we have 3.322 bits of information in a code word of 5 bits. Effectively, then, we have 1.678 "check bits" per word.

The Hamming distances d_{ij} of the 2-out-of-5 code are either 2 or 4. (30 of them are = 2 and 15 of them = 4).

The 4-out-of-8 code has $n = \binom{8}{4} = 70$. This is a sufficient character set for normal alphanumeric data communication and it is in use in some teleprocessing equipment. In this code $I_{max} = \log n = 6.12$ with the minimum redundancy $R = .234$. That is, a redundancy of 1.88 bits per code word.

The reason why the k-out-of-m codes are particularly suited for the detection of burst type errors is that the bit states in data communication are fixed carrier frequencies (beeps of different pitches in voice grade telephone circuits). External electric disturbances such as atmospheric statics also display periodicity to a certain extent. If some of the frequencies in this disturbance have appreciable volume in one of the carrier frequencies it will be received as, say, the bit state 1.

When such a burst lasts several bit times it generates a string of 1's at the receiver producing an invalid k-count, and the error is detected with a high probability.

A special type of parity check codes deserves mentioning here, even though the space does not allow us to discuss their properties. This is the <u>cyclic code</u>. In a cyclic code the valid code words of fixed length are generated through a series of matrix multiplication by the so-called characteristic matrix.

The same operation can be implemented by a physical device (circuitry) called feedback shift register. Same sort of logical circuits serve reception and error detection.

For more details of the cyclic code see R. B. Ash, Chapter 5 or W. W. Peterson, Chapter 8.

All the redundancy codes discussed in this chapter are fixed length codes. In Chapter 3 it was found that an optimum code usually calls for a variable length coding scheme. Are these two requirements incompatible?

In principle not. We could incorporate error checking or correcting capability in a variable length optimum code by the following procedure:

The message, coded in the optimum (binary) code, is divided into blocks of t bits. The boundaries of the blocks need not coincide with the code words. Each of these blocks of t bits are complemented by the c check bits according to the chosen checking system. At reception, after error correction or requested repetition, the redundancy bits are stripped out leaving the original optimum coded message.

Due to some practical difficulties such as the complexity of the coding and decoding equipment these methods are not in general use.

Another compelling reason is that an undetected or uncorrected error, which are unavoidable, mixes up the rest of the message due to a possible shift in the code word boundaries in the optimum code.

Also, codes are normally designed for non-specialized use and the à priori probabilities p_i are unknown.

PART II

CONTINUOUS INFORMATION SYSTEMS

CHAPTER 7

PROPERTIES OF CONTINUOUS CHANNELS

7.1 Continuous Signals

In discrete information systems the channel has discrete properties in two different ways or "dimensions".

First, the characters S_i take always a definite space (or time) t_i, which in most coding systems is an integral multiple of an elementary space such as a bit or an alphabet. We have called this the information cell.

Second, each information cell can take on a value (state) from a finite and discrete set of characters ($n < \infty$).

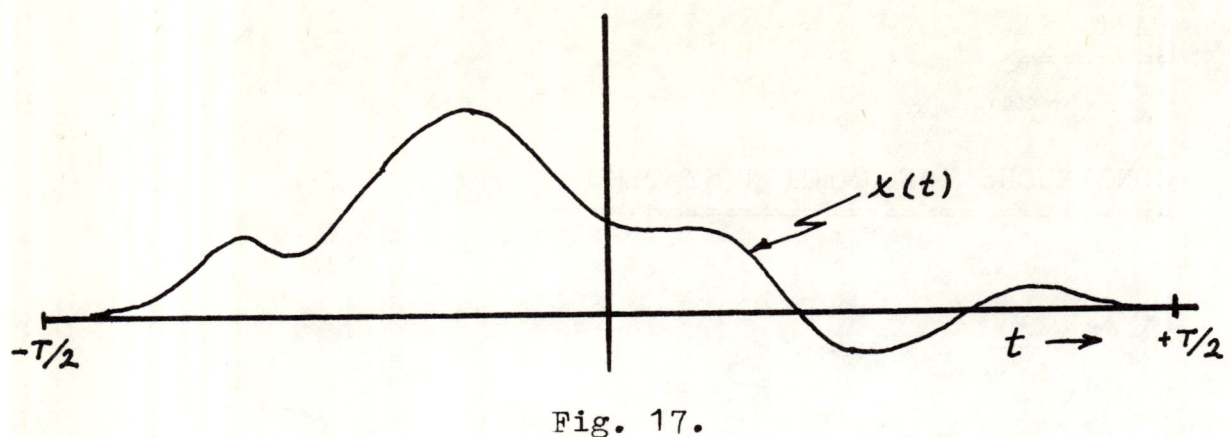

Fig. 17.

We cannot distinguish in a continuous signal such as x(t) of Fig. 17. any natural information cell or character set. Consider x(t), for example, as the amplitude of an electric current in a communication circuit at the instant t of time.

We can, however, associate, by analogy, the time dimension with the information cell (duration) and the amplitude x with the character set (state of the circuit at t).

With no physical constraints on the amplitude x, it seems that x may be in an infinite number of states due to its continuous nature. Thus, with $n = \infty$, the continuous channel would have by definition (5) an infinite information capacity.

In the same way we would be able to define an infinite number of points (cells) of time in a finite time interval T of Fig. 17. with $m = \infty$ rendering an infinite capacity in both dimensions.

In all physically realizable continuous channels we have constraints of one sort or another, which limit the channel capacity and, consequently, the information rate to a finite level.

We are going to discuss in the next paragraph the limitations in the time (space) dimension and in 7.3 the constraints in the amplitude.

7.2 Sampling and Desampling

In most physical systems (in particular electronic equipment) the most significant constraint can be expressed in terms of available **band width** of frequencies. For this reason, the frequency analysis (Fourier analysis, harmonic analysis) is an important mathematical tool in the study of continuous information channels. An appendix on Fourier transform and related mathematical concepts has been included in this book for the benefit of readers not familiar with these methods.

Assume that the continuous signal $x(t)$ of duration T in Fig. 17. is **band limited** by frequency w. That is, $x(t)$, when expressed as a superposition (A18) of its harmonic cosine and sine components, does not have any non-zero components of frequency f higher than w.

If we know, or if we are interested in, only the segment of duration T of x(t), we may define it arbitrarily outside this interval. The simplest definition would be to say that x(t) is zero outside. But, for a definite reason, we define the signal periodic with period T. This is achieved by repeating the interval with period T.

Let us call this function v(t). Then, using definition (A27)

(78) $\qquad v(t) = \text{rep}_T\, x(t)$

The frequency spectrum of the periodic v(t) is discrete (see page A12) with delta peaks at frequencies k/T, $k = 0, \pm 1, \pm 2, \ldots$ This discrete spectrum or Fourier series is by (A32)

(79) $\qquad \text{rep}_T\, x(t) \leftrightarrow V(f) = \frac{1}{T}\, \text{comb}_{1/T}\, X(f)$

where X(f) is the frequency spectrum of the non-periodic x(t) of Fig. 17. Spectrum (79) is illustrated in Fig. 17a.

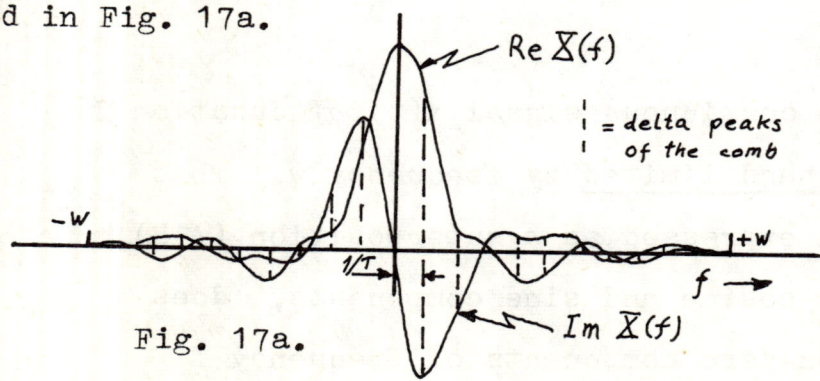

Fig. 17a.

Keeping in mind that the real part Re $X(f)$ or the cosine coefficients a_k are even ($a_{-k} = a_k$) and the imaginary part Im $X(f)$ is odd ($b_{-k} = -b_k$, $b_0 = 0$) it is seen that in the available frequency band $(-w, +w)$ there are $(2wT+1)$ independent values rounded down to the nearest integer. Since the band limit w is seldom very sharp in physical equipment we can, without much more inaccuracy, give this number of "degrees of freedom" as $2wT = g$.

Thus, the frequency spectrum of $v(t)$ defined by (78) is uniquely determined by a set of $g = 2wT$ scalar quantities, that is, a vector of dimension g. On the other hand, this vector determines $v(t)$, and consequently $x(t)$ in interval T, uniquely through (A41). We can say, therefore, that $x(t)$ is also fully determined by g scalar quantities or by a vector of dimension g.

What are the components of this vector?

Let us make $X(f)$ periodic by repeating it at intervals $2w$. Due to the band limit w, these repeated sections of the spectrum do not overlap and by a truncation by $\text{rect}(f/2w)$ (see (A45)) we get the original $X(f)$.

(80) $\qquad X(f) = \left[\text{rep}_{2w} X(f)\right] \text{rect}((f/2w)$

By taking the inverse transform of both sides of the identity (80)

(81)
$$x(t) = \frac{1}{2w} \text{comb}_{1/2w} x(t) \divideontimes 2w \, \text{sinc}(2wt)$$
$$= \text{comb}_{1/2w} x(t) \divideontimes \text{sinc}(2wt)$$
$$= \sum_k x(k/2w) \, \text{sinc}\left[2w(t-k/2w)\right]$$

The last form of (81) indicates that it is the equidistant samples of $x(t)$ with $t = k/2w$ that determine the continuous signal $x(t)$ uniquely.

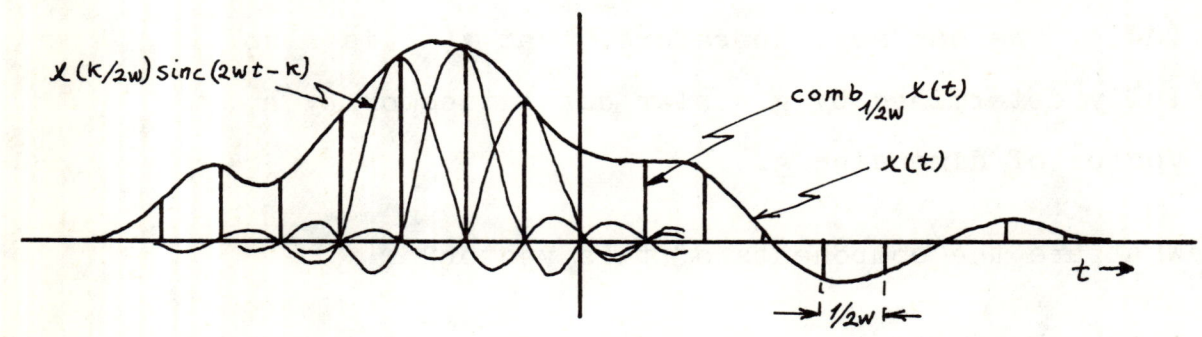

Fig. 18.

Fig. 18. gives an interpretation of (81). Each sampled value $x_k = x(k/2w)$ is replaced by a sinc-curve shifted to point $k/2w$ and multiplied by x_k. $x(t)$ is the sum of all such sinc-curves.

Notice that due to the property $\text{sinc}(m) = 1$ for $m = 1$

and sinc(m) = 0 for all integer $m \neq 0$, the sum curve passes through all sample points x_k.

Summarizing: A continuous signal $x(t)$ limited by a frequency band of frequencies less than w is uniquelly determined by samples taken at constant intervals 1/2w. Values of $x(t)$ can be independently chosen only at intervals equal to or greater than 1/2w. The continuous signal $x(t)$ can be reconstructed without error (interpolated, desampled) by the sinc-interpolation method (81).

This is called the **sampling theorem** of band limited signals.

A practical difficulty arises in applying the interpolation formula in case that $x(t)$ (samples) are not known outside interval T. Expression (81) implies summation over $k = -\infty$ to $k = +\infty$. The "tails" of the sinc's outside the interval also influence the interpolation. In principle, to have full accuracy of $x(t)$ we would need the samples over an infinite time domain.

Now, based on the sampling theorem, we can define the information cell of a band limited continuous channel equal to 1/2w. With other physical constraints we would arrive at a different definition of the cell, but it would be, anyway, a non-zero time segment.

7.3 Gaussian Noise

In the preceding paragraph we assumed implicitly that the samples x_k were indefinitely accurate. In this case every information cell, defined by the sampling theorem, would still have an infinite number of distinguishable states giving an infinite information capacity.

Next, we allow the samples to be inaccurate. This uncertainty of the value of a sample is a form of noise. We consider only a simple form of noise called the Gaussian or white noise with the following properties.

1. Errors of successive samples are statistically independent.
2. The errors are unbiased, that is, they have a zero mean.
3. The errors are normally distributed about the zero mean with a variance σ_N^2.
4. The noise is stationary, that is, the mean or variance do not change with time or depend on the amplitude $x(t)$.

Let us denote the accurate continuous signal by $x(t)$ and the noisy, received signal by $y(t)$. These are analogous to S_i and S_j in the discrete channel.

We denote the error $y(t)-x(t)$ or difference of received and transmitted signal $u(t)$.

(82) $\qquad y(t) = x(t) + u(t)$

The time variable signal $u(t)$ is the noise.

We assume, further, that since the noise is transmitted over the same band limited channel as $x(t)$, it is also band limited and fully determined by the samples $u_k = u(k/2w)$. More precisely, assuming sample errors u_k we can define a continuous $u(t)$ by the sinc-interpolation.

(83) $\qquad u(t) = \sum_k u_k \, \text{sinc}(2wt-k)$

The power of a (electric) signal is proportional to the square of the amplitude. To find the mean noise power P_N we need the integral of $u^2(t)$

(84) $\qquad u^2(t) = \sum_k \sum_j u_k u_j \, \text{sinc}(2wt-k) \, \text{sinc}(2wt-j)$

(85) $\qquad \int_{-\infty}^{\infty} u^2(t)dt = \sum_{i,j} u_k u_j \int_{-\infty}^{\infty} \text{sinc}(2wt-k)\text{sinc}(2wt-j)dt$

It can be shown that the integral in (85) is $= 1/2w$ when $k = j$ and $= 0$ when $k \neq j$. ($\text{sinc}(t)$ is orthogonal with respect to shift by integers)

Hence,

$$(86) \qquad 2w \int_{-\infty}^{\infty} u^2(t)\, dt = \sum_k u_k^2$$

Equation (86) holds for any band limited signal sampled at intervals equal to $1/2w$.

If we extend the integration in (86) over a finite period T, long enough that the integral in (85) is orthogonal with sufficient accuracy we have in the summation of (86) $2wT$ terms, and the mean energy per sample becomes

$$(87) \qquad \frac{a}{2wT} \int_0^T u^2(t)\,dt = a\frac{\sum_k u_k^2}{2wT\ 2w} = a\frac{\overline{u_k^2}}{2w} = E_k$$

where a is a coefficient of proportionality that depends on the unit of energy and $\overline{u_k^2}$ is the mean of u_k^2.

It can be shown (proof not given here, see e.g. P. M. Woodward pp. 37-40.) that $E_k = a\sigma_N^2$. Thus the rate of energy per second, that is, the <u>noise power</u> P_N is, since there are $2w$ samples per second,

$$(88) \qquad P_N = a\, 2w\sigma_N^2$$

The noise power is proportional to available band width w. This is possible only if the noise power is uniformly distributed over all frequencies. By analogy of the white light being a mixture of all (visible) frequencies the Gaussian noise is called often the <u>white noise</u>.

If we choose, for convenience, the units of energy and power such that $a = 1$

(89) $\qquad 2\sigma_N^2 = P_N/w$

and the probability density $p(u)$ of the error u_k is

(90)
$$p(u) = \frac{1}{\sigma\sqrt{2\pi}} \exp(-u^2/2\sigma_N^2)$$
$$= \sqrt{\frac{w}{\pi P_N}} \exp(-wu^2/P_N)$$

according to property 3) on page 112.

7.4 Entropy of Continuous Information

The obvious way of generalizing the entropy of the discrete source

(91) $\qquad H = -\sum_i p_i \log p_i$

to the continuous channel seems to be replacing the discrete probability p_i of character S_i by the probability

(92) $\qquad p(x)\Delta x$

where $p(x)$ is the probability density of $x(t)$ and (92) is the probability of finding $x(t)$ in the interval $(x, x+\Delta x)$. Δx is supposed to be a small increment of x.

By doing this replacement

$$H(x) = -\sum [p(x)\Delta x] \log[p(x)\Delta x]$$

$$= -\sum p(x) \log p(x) \Delta x$$

(93)

$$-\sum p(x) \log(\Delta x) \Delta x$$

If we now let Δx decrease and approach zero the summations are replaced by integrals

(94) $$H(x) = -\int_{-\infty}^{\infty} p(x) \log p(x)\, dx - \int_{-\infty}^{\infty} p(x) \log(dx)\, dx$$

But the second integral in (94) approaches infinity when dx is reduced to zero.

This difficulty is, however, only apparent. The accuracy Δx we want to use in the density expression (92) depends on the noise level. If there were no noise it would be only appropriate to make (92) as accurate as possible by reducing $\Delta x \to 0$. And, as we know from previous discussion, the information rate, and entropy, would be actually infinite. So, mathematically there is nothing wrong in (94) becoming infinite.

In most cases we are not so much interested in the absolute value of the entropy as in its change or the difference of two entropies.

If the two densities p(x) and p(y) of two time variable signals x(t) and y(t) are expressed in the same physical units, say, milliamperes, and Δx and Δy of the respective entropies are reduced at the same rate, the two summations

$$\sum p(x) \log(\Delta x) \Delta x = \log(\Delta x) \sum p(x) \Delta x = \log(\Delta x)$$

and

$$\sum p(y) \log(\Delta y) \Delta y = \log(\Delta y)$$

are always equal and cancel each other.

With this important condition in mind we define the entropy of a continuous signal x(t)

(95) $$H(x) = -\int_{-\infty}^{\infty} p(x) \log p(x)\, dx$$

with $\int_{-\infty}^{\infty} p(x) dx = 1$

Notice that if, for example, x(t) is an electric current and y(t) is the light intensity of a light source their entropies cannot be directly compared. This is because x and y are different physical quantities with different physical units (dimensions).

Notice, also, that H(x) as defined by (95) is a dimensionless number.

In the following we give without proof probability densities p(x) that maximize the entropy (95) under three different constraints.

Case 1. x is limited by amplitude to range 0 to A.

Maximum entropy when $p(x) = \begin{cases} 1/A & 0 \leq x \leq A \\ 0 & \text{else} \end{cases}$

$$H_{max}(x) = - \int_0^A \frac{1}{A} \log(1/A) dx = \log A$$

This is analogous to the uniform discrete distribution in (18).

Case 2. x is non-negative with fixed mean $\bar{x} = 1/\lambda$.

$$\int_{-\infty}^{\infty} x\, p(x)\, dx = \bar{x} = 1/\lambda$$

Maximum entropy when $p(x) = \begin{cases} \lambda e^{-\lambda x} & x \geq 0 \\ 0 & x < 0 \end{cases}$

$$H_{max}(x) = \log(e/\lambda) = \log(e\, \bar{x}) \qquad +)$$

Case 3. x has a fixed mean $\bar{x} = 0$ and variance $= \sigma^2$.

Maximum entropy when x $(0, \sigma)$ normally distributed

$$p(x) = \frac{1}{\sigma \sqrt{2\pi}} \exp(-x^2/2\sigma^2)$$

$$H_{max}(x) = \tfrac{1}{2}\log(2e\pi\sigma^2) \qquad +)$$

+) e is the base of natural logarithms

It is understood that since a logarithm can be defined only for a pure (dimensionless) number the A, $\bar{x}$ and σ^2 in the expressions of H_{max} above refer only to their numerical values. It is seen also from this that the value of entropy depends on selected units.

For example, in Case 2. if $\bar{x}$ = 8 mA, $H_{max}(x)$ = 4.44 If the same $\bar{x}$ is expressed in Amperes $\bar{x}$ = .008 A $H_{max}(x)$ = -5.56.

The distributions p(x) of the three above cases represent the maximum randomness, spread or uncertainty under given conditions.

If x(t) has no physical constraints of amplitude, we could have A = ∞ in Case 1. and an infinite entropy.

7.5. Information Rate and Channel Capacity

We may use one of the two expressions (60) and (62) of information rate in a noisy discrete channel as a starting point in the derivation of the same for a continuous channel.

Let us rewrite (62)

(96) $\qquad I = I(j) - I_i(j)$

$I(j)$, the entropy of the received message, corresponds in channel (82) to

$$(97) \quad H(y) = -\int_{-\infty}^{\infty} p(y) \log p(y) \, dy$$

$I_i(j)$ is the entropy of the conditional probability $p_i(j)$ given by the channel matrix. These entropies are given by expressions (49) and (50).

Probability $p_i(j)$ is replaced by $p_x(y)$ in the continuous channel. This is the conditional probability density of receiving y_k on condition that x_k was transmitted.

In case of Gaussian noise $u(t)$ the received sample y_k is always normally distributed about x_k with variance σ_N^2. Hence, its entropy is the entropy $H(u)$ of the noise distribution (90).

By substitution of these two entropies in (97)

$$(98) \quad I = H(y) - H(u)$$

As the noise, and consequently entropy $H(u)$, is a property of the channel, $H(u)$ is independent of the distributions $p(x)$ and $p(y)$. Under these circumstances the maximum information rate, which equals the channel capacity C, is achieved by maximizing $H(y)$.

In order to have a finite (physically possible) $H(y)$ we have to assume a suitable set of constraints for the received signal $y(t)$. A natural limitation is the mean power P_y. We can write, by the same approach as for the noise on pages 113-114,

$$(99) \qquad P_y = \frac{a}{T} \sum_k y_k^2 = \frac{a}{T} 2wT(\bar{y}^2 + \sigma_y^2)$$

where $\bar{y}$ is the mean of y_k and σ_y^2 is the variance of y_k. Since the mean $\bar{y}$ is consuming energy continuously with time but carries information equal only to one sample it is necessary for the maximum information that $\bar{y} = 0$. Thus, for this case

$$(100) \qquad P_y = a\, 2w\sigma_y^2$$

Under these conditions, according to Case 3. on page 118., the maximum entropy $H_{max}(y)$ will be obtained if y_k are normally distributed with variance σ_y^2.

Now, that $y(t)$ and $u(t)$ are both normally distributed with zero means, we can immediately write the two entropies.

$$(101) \qquad \begin{aligned} H(y) &= \tfrac{1}{2} \log(2e\pi \sigma_y^2) \\ H(u) &= \tfrac{1}{2} \log(2e\pi \sigma_N^2) \end{aligned}$$

and

$$(102) \qquad I_{max} = C = H(y) - H(u) = \log(\sigma_y/\sigma_N)$$

It can be shown that if y_k and u_k are both normally distributed also x_k must be normally distributed due to equation (82), and that also the variances are related by

$$(103) \qquad \sigma_y^2 = \sigma_x^2 + \sigma_N^2$$

where σ_x^2 is the variance of x_k. Analogously with (100) the power of the transmitted signal $x(t)$ is

$$(103) \qquad P_x = a\, 2w\sigma_x^2$$

If we substitute (103) to (102) and express the variances σ_x^2 and σ_N^2 in terms of the respective powers

$$(104) \qquad I_{max} = C = \tfrac{1}{2} \log\left(1 + \frac{P_x}{P_N}\right) \quad \text{bits/sample}$$

The ratio P_x/P_N is called the <u>signal to noise ratio</u>.

Expression (96) gives the information rate <u>per symbol</u>. Therefore, the Equations (98), (102) and (104) are giving the rates and capacities <u>per sample</u>. There are 2w independent samples per second in the band limited signal, which gives us finally

$$(105) \qquad I_{max} = C = w \log\left(1 + \frac{P_x}{P_N}\right) \quad \text{bits/second}$$

This is the capacity of a continuous, band limited channel with Gaussian noise and power limited signal.

Information rates (98) for non-Gaussian noise or some other constraints of the signal $x(t)$ can be, in principle, derived by the same method as above, but they may lead to fairly complex mathematical manipulations.

The Fundamental Theorem of Information Theory (page 97) applies also to the continuous channel. So, for example, with a signal to noise ratio = 1 it is possible to transfer information at a rate $< \frac{1}{2}$ bit per sample (Equation (104)) with an arbitrarily small probability of error by using an appropriate error correcting code. It is, also, seen from (105) that the time rate is directly proportional to the band width w.

CHAPTER 8

DETECTION OF CONTINUOUS SIGNALS

8.1 Principle of Ideal Observer

In this chapter we shall discuss the problem of reception of continuous signals. We shall adopt the same approach as in Chapter 5 with a discrete channel.

The à priori distribution p_i is, as in Chapter 7., replaced by density $p(x)$. Let us add the index k, which refers to the kth sample of the signal, to the à priori distribution. Thus $p(k,x)$ denotes the distribution of $x(t)$ based on observations of $y(t)$ up to the kth sample. If successive samples of $x(t)$ are independent $p(k,x) = p(0,x) = p(x)$.

The noise properties of the channel are again (see page 120) denoted by $p_x(y)$, probability of receiving y when x is transmitted. This equivalent to the channel matrix is called the __likelihood function__ and it is supposed to be stationary with time (same for all sample indices k).

We can write now the two-dimensional probability density $p(k,x,y)$ of the joint occurrence of the kth samples $x_k = x$, $y_k = y$. (Compare with (46))

$$(106) \quad p(k,x,y) = p(k,x)\, p_x(y)$$

This is a function of k only if the knowledge of preceding samples y_j, $j < k$, influences the probability. Starting from the situation after the reception of the k samples of $y(t)$ we can write the probability density $p(k+1,y)$ for the <u>next</u> sample y_{k+1}

$$(107) \quad p(k+1,y) = \int_{-\infty}^{\infty} p(k,x,y)\, dx = \int_{-\infty}^{\infty} p(k,x) p_x(y)\, dx$$

(107) is a predictive probability based on available information up to sample y_k.

To illustrate the development up to now, let us take a specific case. Assume that the signal $x(t)$ and the noise $u(t)$ are normally distributed with zero means and variances σ_x^2 and σ_N^2. Assume that we are just about to start the reception with $k = 0$.

If the noise is stationary and independent of the value (amplitude) of $x(t)$ and it is superimposed on the signal as given by (82) we have obviously

$$(108) \quad p_x(y) = \Big[p(u)\Big]_{u=y-x}$$

That is, the probability density p(u) of the noise amplitude where u has been replaced by y-x. The received value y_k has a distribution centered about the true value x_k with the distribution of the noise error p(u). The fact that no k appears in $p_x(y)$ in (106) or (109) is due to the stationary property of the noise.

If we now substitute the distributions

(109)
$$p(0,x) = \frac{1}{\sigma_x \sqrt{2\pi}} \exp(-x^2/2\sigma_x^2)$$

$$p(u) = \frac{1}{\sigma_N \sqrt{2\pi}} \exp(-u^2/2\sigma_N^2)$$

in (106) observing (108)

(110)
$$p(0,x,y) = \frac{1}{2\pi \sigma_x \sigma_N} \exp\left[-\frac{x^2}{2\sigma_x^2} - \frac{(y-x)^2}{2\sigma_N^2}\right]$$

If we integrate (110) with respect to x in order to get p(1,y) by (107) we see that this is the convolution (see Appendix A) of the two functions (109).

(111)
$$p(1,y) = \frac{1}{\sigma \sqrt{2\pi}} \exp(-y^2/2\sigma^2)$$
where $\sigma^2 = \sigma_x^2 + \sigma_N^2$

Substitution of (108) into (107) shows that p(k+1,y) is the convolution of p(k,x) and p(u) always under condition (82).

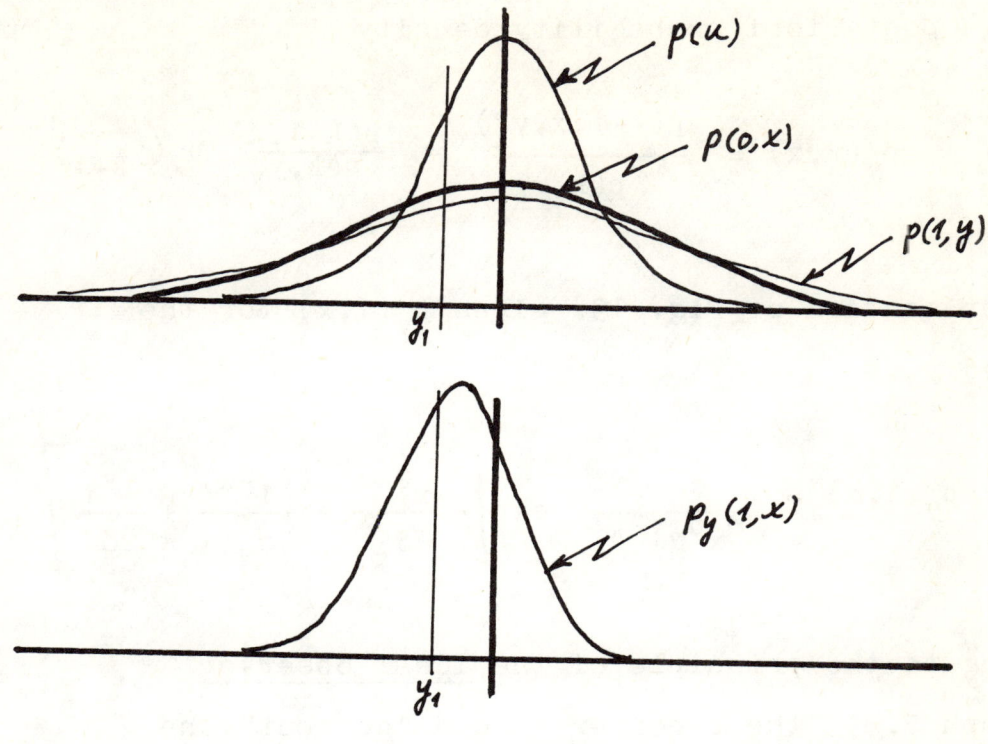

Fig. 19.

The upper section of Fig. 19 illustrates the three density distributions $p(0,x)$, $p(u)$ and $p(1,y)$.

$p(1,y)$ is the distribution of the first received sample y_1 <u>before</u> it has been received (à priori). Assume that y_1 has been received. What is the <u>à posteriori</u> probability $p_y(1,x)$ of the transmitted sample x_1 ?

Apparently (compare with (47))

$$p(1,y_1)p_y(1,x) = p(0,x,y_1)$$

or in general

(112) $$p(k,y_k)p_y(k,x) = p(k-1,x,y_k)$$

and the à posteriori probability density

$$(113) \qquad p_y(k,x) = \frac{p(k-1,x,y_k)}{p(k,y_k)} = \frac{p(k-1,x)}{p(k,y_k)} p_x(y_{k-1})$$

The lower section of Fig. 19. gives $p_y(1,x)$ for the indicated y_1.

$$(114) \qquad p_y(1,x) = \frac{\sigma}{\sigma_x \sigma_N \sqrt{2\pi}} \exp\left[-\frac{x^2}{2\sigma_x^2} - \frac{(y_1-x)^2}{2\sigma_N^2} + \frac{y_1^2}{2\sigma^2}\right]$$

According to the principle of the <u>ideal observer</u> (Paragraph 5.3) the receiver should "correct" the received y_1 to a value x_1' that maximizes the probability (114), that is, the exponent.

Take a numerical case: $\sigma_x^2 = 1$, $\sigma_N^2 = \frac{1}{2}$, (signal to noise ratio = 2) and $y_1 = 1$. Then by (111) $\sigma^2 = 3/2$ and the maximum of (114) is obtained at $x_1' = 2/3$.

Characteristic of the ideal observer is that x_k' is biased towards the maximum of $p(k-1,x)$.

The same applies also to human communication. If you read a comment "The speaker had a horse voice" this sentence has a very low à priori probability and you make the correction "The speaker had a hoarse voice".

In the same way, if you hear an "unbelievable"

(low probability) statement: "A fleet of Martians just landed outside Geneva" your interpretation is that there is something wrong in the information source (transmitter) and you give an error check (do not belive).

This is very important to remember in designing message formats in an information system. Very rare, and usually important, messages (emergency alarms) have to be designed such that there is no close "normal" interpretation of the message.

8.2 Reception of Steady Voltage in Noise

If we assume in the example of the preceding paragraph that successive samples x_k are statistically independent all distributions are identical for all k. That is, knowledge of previous values does not help in the prediction of what is coming next. The ideal receiver would be then a simple device computing $x'_k = 2y_k/3$, which maximizes (114).

Assume, now, that the receiver knows that the m first samples x_k, k = 1,2,...,m, are going to be all equal, but the à priori distribution of the first sample x_1 before y_1 has been received is $p(0,x) = p(x)$. The next sample x_{m+1} will be again drawn independently from distribution p(x) followed by m-1 identical x_k, and so on. This form of signal, illustrated in Fig. 20. will occur in the transmission of discrete voltage levels at a rate 2w/m levels/second. If each level is associated with a symbol S_i of a character set we have a case of transmission of discrete information over a continuous channel (telegraphy) at the rate 2w/m characters/second.

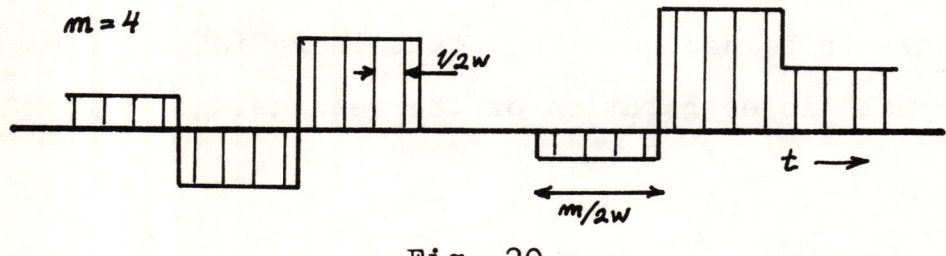

Fig. 20.

Suppose that we have received y_1. After this the probability of x is distributed according to (113).

(115) $\quad p_y(1,x) = \dfrac{p(0,x)}{p(1,y_1)} p_x(y_1)$

But since we know that the next sample x_2 is equal to x_1 the à posteriori probability (115) will be the à priori probability p(1,x) for k = 2, and

(116) $\quad p_y(2,x) = \dfrac{p(1,x)}{p(2,y_2)} p_x(y_2) = p(0,x) \dfrac{p_x(y_1) p(y_2)}{p(1,y_1) p(2,y_2)}$

Since the denominator in (116) is not a function of x, the independent variable of the à posteriori distribution, we can simplify (116) into

(117) $p_y(2,x) = G\, p(x)\, p_x(y_1) p_x(y_2)$

where $p(x) = p(0,x)$ and G is a normalizing coefficient such that

(118) $\int_{-\infty}^{\infty} p_y(2,x)\, dx = 1$

(117) can be now easily generalized to $k = m$

(119) $p_y(m,x) = G\, p(x) \prod_{k=1}^{m} p_x(y_k)$

The ideal observer is one that maximizes (119).

If $p(x)$ and $p(u)$ are those given in (109)

(120) $p_y(m,x) = G\, \exp(-\dfrac{x^2}{2\sigma_x^2} - \dfrac{1}{2\sigma_N^2} \sum_{k=1}^{m} (y_k - x)^2)$

The maximum of (120) is obtained when

(121) $x = \bar{y}_k / (1 + 1/mR)$

where $\bar{y}_k$ is the mean of the m samples

(122) $\bar{y} = \dfrac{1}{m} \sum_{k=1}^{m} y_k$

and R is the signal to noise ratio σ_x^2/σ_N^2.

If $mR \gg 1$ the most probable value of x is the mean $\bar{y}_k$. This is an intuitively acceptable but rather trivial result.

Let us suppose that the continuous channel is used for the transmission of binary information so that $x(t)$ has two possible levels, say, $x(t) = 0$ and $x(t) = 1$. The bit time is equal to m sample times $= m/2w$. The two levels occur independently at probabilities

$$(123) \qquad p(x) = \begin{cases} p_o & \text{for } x = 0 \\ p_1 & \text{for } x = 1 \end{cases}$$

$$p_o + p_1 = 1$$

Assuming Gaussian noise (119) becomes

$$(124) \qquad p_y(m,0) = G\, p_o \exp\left(-\frac{1}{2\sigma_N^2} \sum_{k=1}^{m} (y_k - 0)^2\right)$$

$$p_y(m,1) = G\, p_1 \exp\left(-\frac{1}{2\sigma_N^2} \sum_{k=1}^{m} (y_k - 1)^2\right)$$

The received series of m samples y_k is interpreted as 0 if $p_y(m,0) > p_y(m,1)$ and 1 otherwise. Let us denote the ratio $p_y(m,0)/p_y(m,1) = B$.

$$(125) \qquad B = (p_o/p_1) \exp\left(\frac{1}{2\sigma_N^2} \sum_{k=1}^{m} (1 - 2y_k)\right)$$

The break even point is $B = 1$, which gives

$$(126) \qquad \bar{y}_k = \tfrac{1}{2} + \frac{\sigma_N^2}{m} \ln(p_o/p_1)$$

If the two levels are equal in probability $p_o = p_1$ the decision level is always half way between them ($\bar{y}_k = \tfrac{1}{2}$) otherwise it is closer to the less frequent level.

A numerical case: Assume $p_0 = 4/5$, $p_1 = 1/5$, $R = 3$.
What is the break even point $B = 1$ if $m = 4$?

$$\bar{x} = 0\,(4/5) + 1\,(1/5) = 1/5$$

$$\sigma_x^2 = \frac{4}{5}(0-\frac{1}{5})^2 + \frac{1}{5}(1-\frac{1}{5})^2 = 4/25$$

$$\sigma_N^2 = \sigma_x^2/R = 4/75$$

$$\bar{y}_k = \tfrac{1}{2} + \frac{1}{75}\ln 4 = .519$$

That is, if the mean $\bar{y}_k$ over the four samples is less than .519 the signal is interpreted = 0, otherwise = 1.

The following is a communication system design problem. Assume that p_0, p_1 and R are as above. What should m be, that is, the line speed $2w/m$ bits per second, so that the bit error probability p is less than a specified small probability $\varepsilon = .001$?

The standard deviation σ of the mean $\bar{y}_k$ of m samples is $\sigma = \sigma_N/\sqrt{m}$. If $x = 0$ and $\bar{y}_k$ exceeds (126) (x interpreted = 1) the mean deviates from the distribution mean by an amount q in units of σ such that

$$q\,\frac{\sigma_N}{\sqrt{m}} > \tfrac{1}{2} + \frac{\sigma_N^2}{m}\ln(p_0/p_1)$$

The respective deviation in case x=1 is interpreted erroneously as 0 is r times σ, or

$$r\,\frac{\sigma_N}{\sqrt{m}} > \tfrac{1}{2} - \frac{\sigma_N^2}{m}\ln(p_0/p_1)$$

With the given numerical values

$$q > 2.17\sqrt{m} + .319/\sqrt{m}$$
$$r > 2.17\sqrt{m} - .319/\sqrt{m}$$

The probabilities p_q and p_r of exceeding q and r times the standard deviation (one sided deviation) are found in tables of normal distribution. The total probability of error $p = p_o p_q + p_1 p_r$. These parameters are given in Table 28. It is seen that m = 2 is sufficient to guarantee $p < .001$.

m	q	r	p_q	p_r	p
1	2.49	1.85	.0064	.0322	.0116
2	3.30	2.84	.0005	.0023	.0009
3	3.94	3.58	.0000	.0002	.00004

Table 28.

8.3 Correlation reception

Let us return to the general expression (119) and the special case (120) of the à posteriori probability after the reception of m samples of constant x(t). It was assumed that the sampling is done in accordance with the sampling theorem at intervals 1/2w. In that case we may replace the summation in the exponent of (120) by an integral in the same way as in (86).

(127) $$-\ln(p_y(m,x)/G) = \frac{x^2}{2\sigma_x^2} + \frac{2w}{2\sigma_N^2}\int_0^T (y(t)-x)^2 dt$$

where the range of integration $(0,T)$ is equal to $m/2w$. The maximum of $p_y(m,x)$ will be given by the minimum of (127). This is, of course, the same as (121) with the exception that $\bar{y}_k$ is replaced by the integrated mean

(128) $$\bar{y} = \frac{1}{T}\int_0^T y(t)dt$$

Let us write (127) for an unspecified distribution $p(x)$ and Gaussian noise.

(129) $$-\ln(p_y(m,x)/G) = -\ln p(x) + \frac{w}{\sigma_N^2}\int_0^T (y(t)-x)^2 dt = Z$$

When the square in the integrand is developed we get the first term $y^2(t)$ independent of x. It can be, therefore, thought of as being absorbed in G. The right hand side of (129) becomes then

(130) $$Z = -\ln p(x) + \frac{w}{\sigma_N^2}\int_0^T x^2 dt - \frac{2w}{\sigma_N^2}\int_0^T xy(t)dt$$

Let us assume, next, that x is not a constant level of voltage (or current) over the interval $T = m/2w$ but can take on one out of a (finite) set of possible wave forms $x_i(t)$, $i = 1, 2, \ldots, n$.

These n wave forms constitute now a discrete character set S_i with à priori probabilities $p(x(t)=x_i(t)) = p_i$.

It can be shown that the à posteriori probabilities are obtained by simply replacing the constant levels x by $x_i(t)$ in the integral (129).

$$(131) \quad Z_i = -\ln p_i + \frac{w}{\sigma_N^2} \int_0^T x_i^2(t)dt - \frac{2w}{\sigma_N^2} \int_0^T x_i(t)y(t)dt$$

The ideal observer selects i that minimizes (131).

We notice that the second term of (131) is proportional to the mean energy of $x_i(t)$ over the interval T. The simplest case is one with uniform probabilities $p_i = 1/n$ and mean energies of $x_i(t)$ for all i.

The minimization problem is in this case finding i that maximizes

$$(132) \quad z_i = 2w \int_0^T x_i(t)y(t)dt = \sum_{k=1}^m x_{ik}y_k$$

where x_{ik} is the kth sample of $x_i(t)$.

Expression (132) is recognized as the cross correlation between $x_i(t)$ and $y(t)$. Consequently, this method of reception is called <u>correlation reception</u>.

The following numerical case serves to illustrate how the correlation reception can make the right choice even with a relatively low signal to noise ratio.

k i	1	2	3	4	5
1	0	1	0	1	-1
2	0	0	-1	-1	1
3	1	-1	1	0	0

Table 29.

Matrix x_{ik}

Let $2w = 5/\text{sec}$, $m = 5$, $T = m/2w = 1$ sec, $n = 3$. The three wave forms $x_i(t)$ of equal probability $p_i = 1/3$ are given by the samples in Table 29. and by the approximate continuous curves in Fig. 21.

The signal power P_x is equal to 2w times the mean of $x_i^2(t) = 3/5$ for all i. The noise power $P_N = 2w \sigma_N^2$.

Let us assume a signal to noise ratio $R = \tfrac{1}{2}$, that is, $\sigma_N^2 = 6/5$. Table 30. and the lowest curve in Fig. 21. represent a received signal synthesized by adding to one of the x_{ik} numbers drawn at random

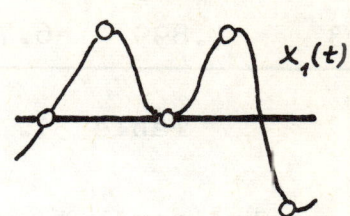
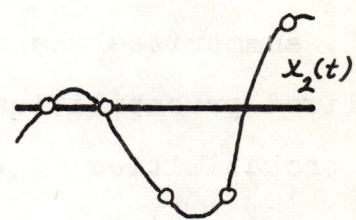
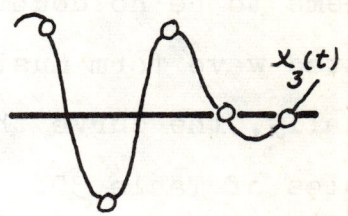
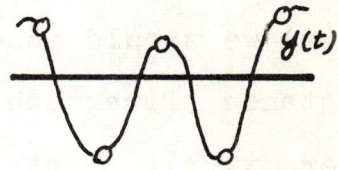

Fig. 21.

k	y_k
1	.572
2	-.978
3	.349
4	-.902
5	.630

Table 30.

i	z_i	e^{z_i}	$p_y(5,i)$
1	-2.510	.082	.008
2	1.183	3.26	.324
3	1.899	6.70	.668

Table 31.

from a normal distribution with $\sigma = \sqrt{6/5}$.

Table 31. summarizes the cross correlations z_i, the unnormalized probabilities e^{z_i} and the final à posteriori probabilities $p_y(m,i)$.

There seems to be no doubt in deciding that the transmitted wave form must have been $x_3(t)$. This is, actually, the curve that was used in synthesizing the samples of Table 30.

It is obvious, that in selecting the set of wave forms $x_i(t)$ we should observe the principle of (Hamming) distance (Paragraph 6.1) from one curve $x_i(t)$ to another $x_j(t)$. That is, the transmitted wave forms should look as different as possible to the receiver. The measure of this "distance" in correlation reception is best defined in terms of the cross correlations between the $x_i(t)$ without noise. Let us call them c_{ij}

$$(133) \qquad c_{ij} = \sum_k x_{ik} x_{jk}$$

i \ j	1	2	3
1	3	-2	-1
2	-2	3	-1
3	-1	-1	3

Table 32.

Matrix c_{ij}

c_{ij} is the matrix product of x_{ik} by its transpose. Table 32. is the c_{ij} of matrix x_{ik} in Table 29.

If we consider $x_i(t)$ as a vector in the "signal space" with the m vector components x_{ik}, k = 1,2,...,m, the cross correlations can be considered as scalar products between the two vectors x_{ik} and x_{jk}, (Compare the m-dimensional signal space with the code space discussed on page 90.) which is proportional to the cosine of the angle between the two vectors.

We get a similar cross correlation expression for discrete code words by multiplying them bit by bit and adding up. Hence, it is seen that the difference between discrete and (band limited) continuous systems is, to a certain extent, only a matter of different approach. The basic difference is that the levels of x_{ik} are not limited to fixed discrete levels, but can be chosen (within physical constraints) from a continuum of values.

We recognize that when $c_{ii} = \sum_k x_{ik}^2$ is constant as in our example we have a case analogous to the k-out-of-m code.

The principle of minimum distance between two wave

forms will be based on the difference

(134) $\quad d_{ij} = c_{ii} - c_{ij}$

It is seen in Table 33. that the minimum distance in the example case is 4.

(Notice, (134) is not equal to the Hamming distance defined on page 90.)

i \ j	1	2	3
1	0	5	4
2	5	0	4
3	4	4	0

Table 33. Matrix d_{ij}

Suppose now, in the example, that the transmitted wave form was $x_s(t)$ and the received signal $y(t) = x_s(t) + u(t)$. The sampled cross correlation (132) will be then

$$(135) \quad \begin{aligned} z_i &= \sum_k x_{ik}(x_{sk} + u_k) \\ &= c_{is} + \sum_k x_{ik} u_k \\ &= c_{is} + N_i \end{aligned}$$

where u_k are the noise samples from a normal distribution and statistically independent.

The N_i are weighted sums of these samples and also normally distributed with zero mean and variance

$$\sigma_{N_i}^2 = c_{ii} \sigma_N^2$$

All N_i, however, are not mutually independent. By taking the sum of N_i over all i

$$(136) \quad \sum_i N_i = \sum_k u_k \sum_i x_{ik} = \sum_k u_k b_k$$

where b_k are the column sums of matrix x_{ik}, Table 29. In the example we find $b_1 = 1$ and $b_k = 0$ when $k \neq 1$. That is,

$$\sum_k N_i = u_1$$

The same approach can be used to estimate error probabilities in correlation reception. An error occurs if in (135) any of the $z_i = c_{is} + N_i$ ($i \neq s$) is higher than $z_s = c_{ss} + N_s$. In the example $s = 3$. Thus, we have an error if

$$c_{13} + N_1 = -1 + N_1 > c_{ss} + N_s = 3 + N_3$$
or
$$c_{23} + N_2 = -1 + N_2 > c_{ss} + N_s = 3 + N_3$$
or both

That is

$$(137) \text{ or} \quad \begin{aligned} N_1 - N_3 &> c_{33} - c_{13} = d_{13} = 4 \\ N_2 - N_3 &> c_{33} - c_{23} = d_{23} = 4 \end{aligned}$$

or both

But the two differences can be written

$$(138) \quad \begin{aligned} N_1 - N_3 &= \sum_k (x_{1k} - x_{3k}) u_k \\ N_2 - N_3 &= \sum_k (x_{2k} - x_{3k}) u_k \end{aligned}$$

The vectors in the parentheses are row differences of matrix x_{ik} and they are easily obtained. From Table 29.

(139)
$$x_{1k} - x_{3k} = -1, 2, -1, 1, -1$$
$$x_{2k} - x_{3k} = -1, 1, -2, -1, 1$$

In general $N_i - N_s$ is normally distributed with zero mean and variance

(140)
$$\sigma_N^2 \sum_k (x_{ik} - x_{sk})^2$$

For the example both differences have variances = $8\sigma_N^2$ = 48/5, but they are not independent. Fig. 22. tries to illustrate this in a three-dimensional case (m = n = 3).

x_{ik} are vectors and (139) are differences of two such <u>signal vectors</u>. u_k constitutes a random <u>noise vector</u>. Expressions (135) and (138) are scalar products between the noise vector and signal vectors or their differences.

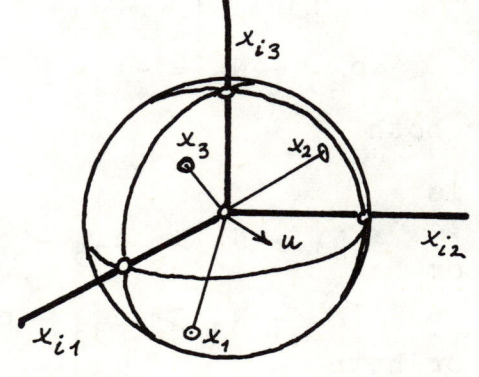

Fig. 22.

If this dependence is taken in consideration the two cases (138) seldom occur simultaneously and the total error probability with variance 48/5 and distance 4 is found to be .197.

Up to now we have treated only the case that all possible wave forms $x_i(t)$ have an equal mean power and equal probabilities p_i.

Differences in the mean energies call for only a simple correction in z_i. The only thing we have to do (see Equation (131)) is to subtract the sum

$$w \int_0^T x_i^2(t)dt = \tfrac{1}{2} \sum_k x_{ik}^2 = \tfrac{1}{2} c_{ii}$$

which now depend on i.

The problem of detection becomes more serious if the à priori probabilities p_i are not equal. In the previous cases the noise power, that is, σ_N^2 does not appear in the criterion z_i of detection. Now, the correction term of z_i as defined by (132) would be $\sigma_N^2 \ln p_i$.

What is the effect of a wrong assumption concerning the noise power or, which is equivalent, the signal to noise ratio?

We notice first that $\ln p_i$ is always negative and increases in absolute value with decreasing p_i. If the noise power is assumed too high it results in an unproportionately strong reduction of z_i of the less frequent signals and an increased error rate in their detection. Conversely, a too low estimation of the noise power increases the errors of the more frequent signals.

It has become evident from the preceding error analysis that, in order to minimize the total error rate, the wave forms should be chosen such that the distances

(141) $\quad d'_{ij} = c'_{ii} - c'_{ij}$

with

(142) $\quad c'_{ij} = \sigma_N^2 \ln p_i - \tfrac{1}{2} \sum_k x_{ik}^2 + \sum_k x_{ik} x_{jk}$

are as high as possible for $i \neq j$. ($d'_{ii} = 0$)

The criterion of reception z'_i (compare (132)) becomes

(143) $\quad z'_i = \sigma_N^2 \ln p_i - \tfrac{1}{2} \sum_k x_{ik}^2 + \sum_k x_{ik} y_k$

In case of an analog reception device the summations in (142) and (143) are replaced by appropriate integrals.

Characteristic of the correlation reception is that it is necessary to know the transmitted set of wave forms $x_i(t)$ and their à priori probabilities p_i. If p_i are not equal we have to know, in addition, the approximate signal to noise ratio R at the receiver.

This can be expressed by a statement:
"You cannot find the signal in noise if you do not know what you are looking for."

CHAPTER 9

INFORMATION FILTERS

Discrete (numerical) or continuous (analog) filtering of information can be considered almost as a science in itself and often not considered as part of information theory. Due to the importance of the topic in data processing and since much of the theory can be directly based on the concepts covered in previous chapters a brief introduction to the subject will be given in this chapter.

9.1 Convolution Filter

A filter, in a broad sense, is understood as a process having a noisy signal as input and giving out another signal (time series) that is as close as possible to the original signal without noise. This is a selective process that destroys noise but retains the required information.

Now, let us look again at the correlation reception (Paragraph 8.3), which is also an information filter by the above definition. A succesful reception requires that the receiver is synchronized with the transmitter.

For example, assume that we have a sequence of wave forms of Fig. 21., say, $x_3(t), x_3(t), x_1(t)$. This message would be equal to the following transmitted 15 samples

$$\cdots \overbrace{1\ \text{-}1\ 1\ 0\ 0}^{x_3}\ \overbrace{1\ \text{-}1\ 1\ 0\ 0}^{x_3}\ \overbrace{0\ 1\ 0\ 1\ \text{-}1}^{x_1} \cdots$$

If the receiver were leading in phase by one sample time it would consider the two groups of samples

$$0\ 1\ \text{-}1\ 1\ 0$$
$$0\ 0\ 1\ 0\ 1$$

as sampled wave forms $x_i(t)$. It is evident that the message would be completely distorted. The most probable interpretations of the above two groups would be $x_1(t)$ and $x_3(t)$ (highest correlation).

Is it possible to design the set of wave forms $x_i(t)$ such that the receiver would be insensitive to errors of synchronization (phase shifts)?

To answer this question, let us consider a noisy signal in which we have supressed all other wave forms except one, say, $x_i(t)$. That is, $x_j(t) \equiv 0$ for $j \neq i$, Fig. 23.

Consider, further, only one of the $x_i(t)$ in the sequence, one starting at time τ_1, which is unknown to the receiver.

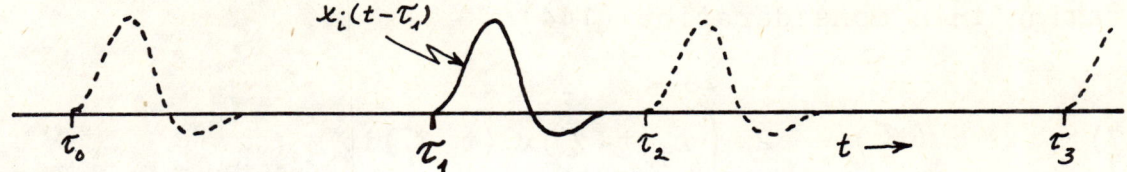

Fig. 23.

The received signal y(t) is then in the continuous form

(144) $y(t) = x(t) + u(t) = x_i(t-\tau_1) + u(t)$

and in the discrete form, assuming that τ_1 is an integral multiple of the sampling interval

(145) $y_k = x_{i,k-j} + u_k \quad ; \quad j = 2w\tau_1$

If we now allow for the unknown time shift by introducing it in (132) as a variable τ, the reception criterion z_i becomes (by neglecting at first the two first terms of (131)) a function of τ or the discrete index s

(146) $z_i(\tau) = 2w \int_{-\infty}^{\infty} x_i(t-\tau)y(t)dt = \sum_k x_{i,k-s} y_k = z_i(s)$

where $s = 2w\tau$. The limits of integration and the range of summation in (146) should be from τ to $\tau +T$ and from k = s to k = s+m, but if we define $x_i(t) = 0$ outside the range (0,T) we can have formally infinite limits.

By taking into consideration (144)

$$(147) \quad z_i(\tau) = 2w \int_{-\infty}^{\infty} x_i(t-\tau) x_i(t-\tau_1) dt + 2w \int_{-\infty}^{\infty} x_i(t-\tau) u(t) dt$$

If we compare the second integral of (147) with the definition (A19) (Appendix A) of the convolution we see that it can be written as $x_i(-\tau) \not\star u(\tau)$. The first integral is, by the same token, also a convolution. In order to simplify notations, let us denote the difference $\tau - \tau_1 = v$. If the noise is stationary, as we have assumed, a time shift generated by replacing t by t- τ_1 in u(t) has no effect.

By these notations (147) becomes

$$(148) \quad z_i(\tau_1 + v) = 2w\, x_i(-v) \not\star x_i(v) + 2w\, x_i(-v) \not\star u(v)$$

v is a time variable, which can be taken as the "error" in the assumed time shift τ against the actual shift τ_1.

We notice from (147) that the first convolution in (148) is the (unnormalized) correlation of $x_i(t)$ with itself shifted by an amount v (autocorrelation). This assumes always the maximum value with v = 0. The maximum value is according to notation (133) equal to c_{ii}, when multiplied by 2w.

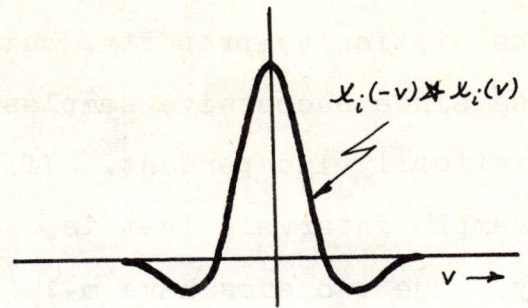

Fig. 24.

Fig. 24. represents $x_1(-v) \not\star x_1(v)$ of $x_1(t)$ in Fig. 21. This convolution of a function by itself reflected about the ordinate axis is sometimes called the <u>convolution square</u> of the function.

We see now that (146), which is the convolution of $y(t)$ by $x(-t)$, reaches its maximum value, apart from the noise term, equal to c_{ii} at $\tau = \tau_1$. Hence, (146) is a sufficient criterion of detection for one single $x_i(t)$ in absence of synchronization between the transmitter and the receiver.

What are the properties of the noise term

(149) $$N_i(\tau) = 2w \, x_i(-\tau) \not\star u(\tau) = \sum_k x_{i,k-s} u_k$$

First we see, since the mean of $u(t)$ is zero, by (A25) that the mean of (149) is also zero. Further, in case of Gaussian noise, (149) is a weighted sum of m independent samples from a normal distribution with variance σ_N^2. This sum is also normally distributed with variance

$$\sigma_{N_i}^2 = c_{ii} \, \sigma_N^2$$

Noise (149) has also the stationary property, but it is **not** Gaussian noise since successive samples of $N_i(\tau)$ are not statistically independent. If τ is advanced by one sample interval, that is, s is increased by unity, the two sums have m-1 u_k samples equal (with different weights $x_{i,k-s}$). We call (149) **filtered noise**.

Finally, we write (146)

$$z_i(\tau) = 2w \; x_i(-\tau) \star y(\tau)$$

(151)
$$= 2w \; x_i(-v) \star x_i(v) + N_i(\tau)$$

$$v = \tau - \tau_1$$

According to (A23) the frequency spectrum of $z_i(\tau)$ (Fourier transform) is (see also (A10))

(152) $\quad z_i(\tau) \leftrightarrow 2w \; X_i^*(f) \; Y(f)$

where $X_i(f)$ and $Y(f)$ are the transforms of $x_i(\tau)$ and $y(\tau)$, and the asterix denotes complex conjugate.

This process (152) whereby the harmonic (frequency) components of the signal are multiplied by a factor $X(f)$, which varies with the frequency, is called a **filtering** process. If $X_i(f)$, the filter function, is complex the amplitude as well as the phase of $Y(f)$ are changed.

Filtering process in the frequency domain corresponds to a convolution in the time domain.

The filter function that constitutes the ideal observer for a wave form $x_i(t-\tau_1)$ with an unknown time shift τ_1 is the complex conjugate of the Fourier transform of the same wave form.

Up to now we have assumed that there is only one wave form $x_i(t)$ extending from τ_1 to $\tau_1 + T$ and the signal $x(t) = 0$ outside this interval. If there are several such wave forms (non-overlapping) starting at instants $\tau_1, \tau_2, \tau_3, \ldots$ the criterion of detection (151) shows peaks (maxima) approximately equal to c_{ii} at values of τ equal to the starting moments. Thus, they can be all detected, assuming a sufficiently high signal to noise ratio, by means of the same filter or reception process.

Next, assume that the signal $x(t)$ is a mixture of all possible wave forms $x_i(t)$, $i = 1, 2, \ldots, n$, but we want only to detect one particular type, say, those that have $i = 3$ and to have the receiver insensitive to the others.

To see how this can be achieved let us take (151) without the noise term and assume that $y(t)$ is a superposition of all possible $x_i(t)$ with appropriate time shifts. In that case $z_i(\tau)$ will be a superposition of respective convolutions with $x_i(-\tau)$.

Now, if all convolutions $x_i(-\tau) * x_j(\tau) \equiv 0$ for $i \neq j$ the receiver would only "hear" $x_i(t)$'s.

But this condition, expressed in the frequency domain, is

(153) $\quad X_i^*(f)X_j(f) \equiv 0 \quad$ when $i \neq j$

That is, the "passing" frequency bands of filter functions corresponding to $x_j(t)$ do not overlap those of $x_i(t)$. If we extend this principle to hold between all pairs i,j we can apply the same detection principle to all wave forms.

The simplest way to guarantee (153) very closely is to make $x_i(t)$ segments of sine waves of different frequencies, for example, 50, 100, and 150 cycles per second.

The Fourier transform of a sine wave of duration T is found by applying (A45). The spectrum of $\sin 2\pi f_i t$ has delta peaks at $\pm f_i$ and we get the truncated form

(154) $\quad X_i(f) = \dfrac{\sin[\pi T(f-f_i)]}{f - f_i}$

The ideal band pass filters for the three above carrier waves would look by (154) approximately like those in Fig. 25.

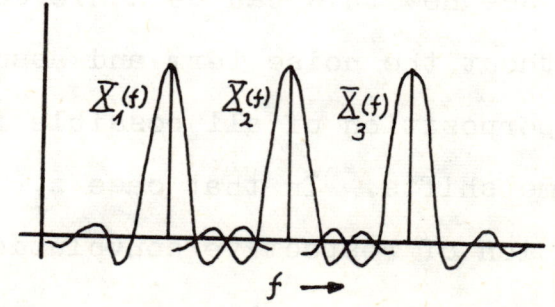

Fig. 25.

By this method the available channel capacity can be divided in sub channels each utilizing a narrow band width of the total available frequency band. In our example the different wave forms never overlapped one another, but since the individual filters $X_i(f)$ pass only one specific wave form there is no reason why we could not superimpose different wave forms. This is how different radio and TV channels utilize the common communication medium without causing interference in receivers tuned to filter only the required frequency band.

If the three frequencies $f_1 = 50$, $f_2 = 100$, $f_3 = 150$, taken as examples on page 152, are used to transmit

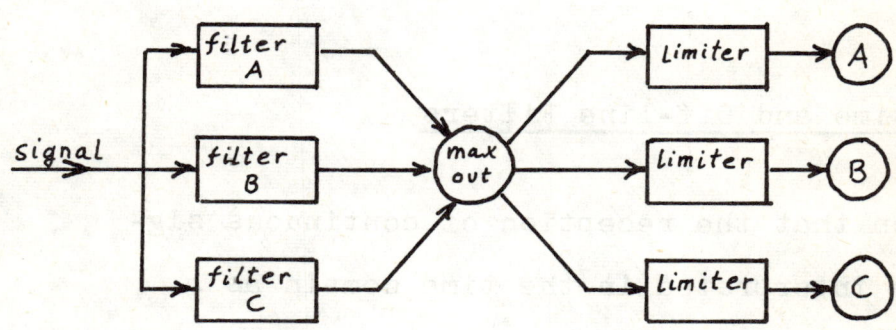

Fig. 26.

a message in a ternary code $S_1 = A$, $S_2 = B$, $S_3 = C$ the receiver consists of three parallel band pass filters of type (154) tuned to respective frequencies f_i. The filters are followed by a comparator that selects the highest $z_i(\tau)$. (Assume all c_{ii} equal) The comparator is followed by limiters set to pass a $z_i(\tau)$ only if it exceeds a threshold value close to c_{ii}. Pulses passing the limiter register the appropriate character.

If the highest $z_i(\tau)$ does not pass the limiter it can be interpreted as no transmission or a transmission error due to noise. Selection of the threshold level is based on an error analysis so that the two kinds of errors

1) A character registered when there was none (threshold too low)
2) Character rejected due to noise (threshold too high)

are properly balanced.

9.2 Real-time and Off-line Filters

We have seen that the reception of continuous signals can be interpreted in the time domain as a convolution operation or in the frequency domain as the multiplication by the filter function.

In this paragraph we are going to discuss some constraints in the design of filters imposed by time.

Let us reconsider the criterion of reception (146) of the convolution reception in the sampled form.

$$(155) \qquad z(s) = \sum_{k=s}^{s+m} q_{k-s} y_k \quad ; \quad \begin{array}{l} s = 2w \\ k = 2wt \end{array}$$

where $q(t)$, its samples q_k and transform $Q(f)$ represent in general a filter, not necessarily $x_i(t)$.

We recognize (155) as a weighted sum of m consequtive samples of the <u>time series</u> y_k with weights q_{k-s}. The resulting time series $z(s)$ is a filtered or <u>smoothed</u> series.

Usually the weights are normalized so that they add up to unity

$$(156) \qquad \sum_{k=0}^{m-1} q_k = 1$$

Then, by equation (A25), the original series y_k and the smoothed series $z(s)$ have same mean, and the filter has no amplifying or attenuating effect on the mean.

By writing (155) in the form

$$(157) \qquad z(s) = \sum_{k=0}^{m-1} q_k y_{s+k}$$

we notice that the smoothed value $z(s)$ at the moment s requires that we know the original series m-1 samples into the <u>future</u> (from y_s to y_{s+m-1}).

If we are processing (smoothing) a time series such as daily production data of a manufacturing plant over the period of the past year and having the whole series available when we start the process, this is no problem. (off-line filter)

On the other hand, if we want to do the smoothing in <u>real-time</u>, that is, at the end of this day, having today's production data y_k available, we would like to know also the smoothed value $z(s)$ immediately, we could not do it with the filter of (157).

The reason why we have the weights q_k in (157) running to the future derives back to page 146, where we defined τ_1 as the <u>starting</u> moment of the wave form $x_i(t)$. Hence, also the peak of $z_i(\tau) = c_{ii}$ should occur at $\tau = \tau_1$, that is, at the <u>beginning</u> of the wave form $x_i(t)$. This would be a predictive filter if it could be physically (or computationally) implemented.

We have a non-predictive filter if τ_1 is defined as the end moment of $x_i(t)$ and, in that case, (157) would be

$$(158) \qquad z(s) = \sum_{k=-m+1}^{0} q_k \, y_{s+k}$$

This is, however, just a mathematical "trick" that

does not change the nature of the problem. In (157) we can tell the beginning of the wave form after a delay of m-1 sample times; in (158) we detect the end of the same event with no delay, which is, in effect, exactly the same thing.

The filtering or smoothing process in the form of the weighted sum (157) is called a <u>numerical filter</u>.

9.3. <u>Filtering Redundant Time Series</u>

Up to now we have always assumed that the sampling of the continuous signal $y(t)$ is done at intervals $1/2w$ where w is the highest frequency that occurs in the signal $x(t)$. In this case successive samples are statistically independent.

Assume now that the sampling interval is shortened to $1/2w'$ such that $w' > w$. The successive samples in this time series are no longer independent and this introduces redundacy in the information (see Paragraph 4.3).

How can we use this redundancy for improving accuracy or reliability of the information received?

This can be demonstrated in the simplest way by considering the situation in the frequency domain.

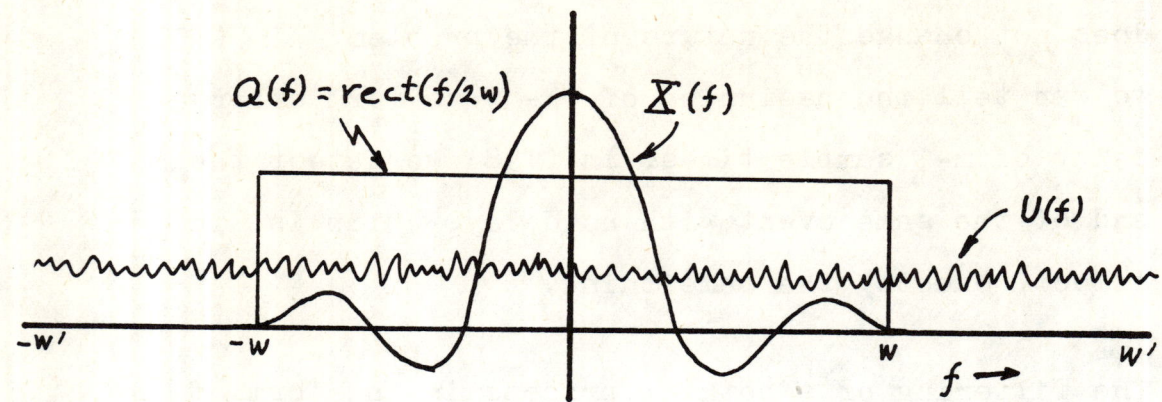

Fig. 27.

According to the sampling theorem (page 111), interpreted in reverse, we are observing all frequencies of y(t) with the new sampling interval $1/2w'$ up to the frequency $f = w'$. In case of Gaussian noise the noise power P_N is uniformly distributed over the whole available band $(-w', +w')$ but the signal only from $-w$ to $+w$, Fig. 27.

If we apply to y_k an ideal low pass filter

(159) $q(t) \leftrightarrow Q(f) = \text{rect}(f/2w)$

we are not causing any distortion to the signal but reducing the noise power by factor $w/w' < 1$.

Filter function (159) corresponds to the numerical filter

(160) $q(t) = 2w \, \text{sinc}(2wt)$

By replacing t by $t = k/2w'$ and normalizing by (156) the weights q_k are

$$(161) \qquad q_k = \frac{w}{w'} \cdot \text{sinc}(kw/w') = \frac{\sin(\pi kw/w')}{\pi k}$$

$\lvert k \rvert$	q_k
0	.333
1	.276
2	.138
3	0
4	-.069
5	-.055
6	0
7	.040
8	.035

Table 34.

Table 34. gives the numerical values of (161) for the case $w/w' = 3$ and $\lvert k \rvert \leq 8$.

It is seen that (161) extends from an infinite past $k = -\infty$ to the infinite future $k = \infty$. In practice the q_k can be truncated at a suitable k when q_k has diminished to an insignificant level.

This numerical filter is less suitable for real-time filtering due to the symmetry about k = 0. All real filter functions have this property.

Let us see what the filter functions of two commonly used numerical real-time filters are.

<u>Floating average</u>. The weights q_k for this filter are if the average is based on m most recent samples

$$(162) \qquad q_k = \begin{cases} 1/m & -m+1 \leq k \leq 0 \\ 0 & \text{else} \end{cases}$$

This comes from the continuous function

$$(163) \qquad q(t) = \frac{1}{m} \text{rect}\left(\frac{2w't + m-1}{m}\right)$$

By applying equation (A3) we get the filter function

$$(164) \qquad Q(f) = \frac{1}{2w'} \text{sinc}(mf/2w') \exp(\pi i \frac{m-1}{w'} f)$$

The sinc-factor determines the amplitude and the exponent function with an imaginary argument the phase.

Exponential smoothing. The weights q_k are (unnormalized)

$$(165) \qquad q_k = \begin{cases} \exp(ak) & k \leq 0 \\ 0 & k > 0 \end{cases} \qquad a = \text{const.}$$

And

$$(166) \qquad q(t) = \begin{cases} \exp(2w'at) & t \leq 0 \\ 0 & t > 0 \end{cases}$$

and the filter function

$$(167) \qquad Q(f) = \frac{1}{2aw' - 2\pi i f}$$

The amplitude of (167) is

$$(168) \qquad |Q(f)| = \frac{1}{\sqrt{(2aw')^2 + (2\pi f)^2}}$$

Even if we have called these real-time filters since they use samples only from the past they still have in effect a delay between s and k in z(s) and y_k. So, for example, we would rather associate the floating average (162) with a time s - m/2, the center of the samples. (165) introduces in the same way a mean delay of $1/2aw'$.

This effective delay is equal to the distance of the center of gravity of q_k from the origin $k = 0$.

$$(169) \qquad \text{delay} = -\frac{1}{2w'} \sum_k k\, q_k = D$$

Since we cannot avoid this delay with $q_k = 0$ for positive k we could make the following compromise.

Select a suitable even and real filter function $Q(f)$ such as (159). Take the inverse transform $q(t)$, which is an even function ($q(-t) = q(t)$). Define an acceptable delay D. Find a point t_o such that

$$(170) \qquad \int_{-\infty}^{t_o} (t_o - t) q(t) dt = D \int_{-\infty}^{t_o} q(t) dt$$

Truncate the part $t > t_o$. This truncated function has the center of gravity at the point $t_o - D$. The numerical filter (normalize if necessary)

$$(171) \qquad q_k = \begin{cases} \tfrac{1}{2} q(t_o) & k = 0 \\ q(t_o + k/2w') & k < 0 \end{cases}$$

is approximately equal to filter function $Q(f)$ with a delay D.

What is the most suitable filter function?

We could argue in the following way. The relative amount of information carried by a harmonic component of frequency f is proportional to its amplitude X(f) in the signal x(t). For example, very low and very high pitch harmonics in a human voice have a relatively low amplitude. They can be filtered out without much impairing intelligibility. The medium range of pitch, which have higher amplitudes, are, on the contrary, essential for the understanding.

Thus it seems that the best filter would be one that has Q(f) proportional to X(f) or, if we leave the normalization to the end

$$(172) \qquad |Q(f)| = |X(f)|$$

This finding is in a good agreement with (146) and (154).

If the numerical filtering or smoothing is done by hand calculations expressions such as (158) require a good amount of tedious work. Therefore such simple filters as the floating average and exponential smoothing (which can be reduced to two additions and one multiplication per sample) have gained a high popularity.

But if the same work is done on a computer simple array operations (158) present no problems. Also, from the point of wiev of computation time, it is only the number of non-zero q_k that is significant, not their values (using a given number of digits).

Therefore, when analyzing redundant time series on a computer, it is in most cases worth the effort to find the numerical filter best suited to the case.

Very often numerical filters used in computer programs are simulating some common analog filters such as low pass filters with resistors, capacitors and induction coils. But since a digital computer has a full freedom of choice of q_k there is no reason to carry the limitations of these physical devices to the computer programs.

REFERENCES FOR FURTHER STUDY

1. R. B. ASH, Information Theory, Interscience, 1965.

2. R. B. BLACKMAN, Data Smoothing and Prediction, Addison-Wessley, 1965.

3. L. BRILLOUIN, Science and Information Theory, Academic Press, 1956.

4. BROCKWAY et al., Current Trends in Information Theory, Univ. of Pittsburgh Press, 1953.

5. R. G. BROWN, Smoothing, Forecasting and Prediction of Discrete Time Series, Prentice-Hall, 1963.

6. C. CHERRY, On Human Communication, MIT Press, 1966.

7. DOCKX, BERNAYS, Information and Prediction in Science, Academic Press, 1965.

8. W. MEYER-EPPLER, Grundlagen und Anwendungen der Informationstheorie, Springer, 1959.

9. W. W. PETERSON, Error Correcting Codes, Wiley, 1961.

10. J. R. PIERCE, Symbols, Signals and Noise, Harper, 1961.

11. G. RAISBECK, Information Theory, MIT Press, 1965.

12. F. M. REZA, An Introduction to Information Theory, McGraw-Hill, 1961.

13. L. SACCO, Manuel de Cryptographie, Payot, 1951.

14. C. E. SHANNON, W. WEAVER, The Mathematical Theory of Communication, Univ. of Illinois Press, 1959.

15. L. S. SCHWARTZ, Principles of Coding, Filtering, and Information Theory, Spartan Books, 1963.

16. I. SELIN, Detection Theory, Princeton Univ. Press, 1965.

17. N. WIENER, Extrapolation, Interpolation, and Smoothing of Stationary Time Series, Wiley, 1949.

18. P. M. WOODWARD, Probability and Information Theory with Applications to Radar, Pregamon, 1953.

APPENDIX A

FOURIER TRANSFORM AND RELATED CONCEPTS

A1. Definitions and Basic Properties

The Fourier transform $F(x(t))$ of function $x(t)$ is denoted by the capital letter $X(f)$ and defined by

$$(A1) \quad F(x(t)) = X(f) = \int_{-\infty}^{\infty} x(t) \exp(-2\pi i f t) \, dt$$

where t is the independent variable (time) of $x(t)$, f is the independent variable (frequency) of the transform $X(f)$, $\exp(z) = e^z$ = exponential function, $i = \sqrt{-1}$ = the imaginary unit.

Operation (A1) is linear, that is,

$$(A2) \quad \begin{aligned} F(x(t)+y(t)) &= F(x(t)) + F(y(t)) \\ &= X(f) + Y(f) \\ F(ax(t)) &= a\, F(x(t)) = a\, X(f) \quad ; \quad a = \text{const.} \end{aligned}$$

Following properties are directly derivable from (A1) where the relationship of $x(t)$ and its transform $X(f)$ is denoted by $x(t) \leftrightarrow X(f)$

$$(A3) \quad x\left(\frac{t-b}{a}\right) \leftrightarrow a\, X(af) \exp(-2\pi i f b)$$

a and b constants

$$\text{(A4)} \qquad X(0) = \int_{-\infty}^{\infty} x(t)\, dt$$

By applying the Euler's formula

$$\text{(A5)} \qquad \exp(-2\pi i f t) = \cos 2\pi f t - i \sin 2\pi f t$$

and assuming $x(t)$ real we have for the real component Re and the imaginary component Im of $X(f)$

$$\text{(A6)} \qquad \begin{aligned} \operatorname{Re} X(f) &= \int_{-\infty}^{\infty} x(t) \cos 2\pi t f\, dt \\ \operatorname{Im} X(f) &= -\int_{-\infty}^{\infty} x(t) \sin 2\pi t f\, dt \end{aligned}$$

Any function $x(t)$ can be divided into its even $x_e(t)$ and odd $x_o(t)$ component

$$\text{(A7)} \qquad \begin{aligned} x_e(t) &= \tfrac{1}{2}\left[x(t) + x(-t)\right] \\ x_o(t) &= \tfrac{1}{2}\left[x(t) - x(-t)\right] \end{aligned}$$

and by parity considerations (A6) can be written

$$\text{(A8)} \qquad \begin{aligned} \operatorname{Re} X(f) &= 2\int_{0}^{\infty} x_e(t) \cos 2\pi t f\, dt \\ \operatorname{Im} X(f) &= -2\int_{0}^{\infty} x_o(t) \sin 2\pi t f\, dt \end{aligned}$$

The integrals in (A8) are called the cosine and sine transforms respectively.

In case $x(t)$ is non-zero only for $t \geqslant 0$, $x_e = x_o = \tfrac{1}{2} x$.

From (A7)

(A9)
$$x(t) = x_e(t) + x_o(t)$$
$$x(-t) = x_e(t) - x_o(t)$$

Hence by (A8)

(A10) $x(-t) \leftrightarrow X^*(f)$ = complex conjugate of $X(f)$

A2. Delta Function

The Dirac's delta function $d(t)$ or the unit peak function is defined by the two simultaneous equations

(A11)
$$d(t) = 0 \quad \text{when} \quad t \neq 0$$
$$\int_{-\infty}^{\infty} d(t)\, dt = 1$$

$d(t)$ can be obtained through a limit process from any function with a finite integral from $-\infty$ to $+\infty$ and $x(-\infty) = x(+\infty) = 0$. One such function is the Gaussian

(A12) $d(t) = \lim\limits_{\sigma \to 0} \dfrac{1}{\sigma\sqrt{2\pi}} \exp(-t^2/2\sigma^2)$

The Fourier transform of the Gaussian is

(A13) $\dfrac{1}{\sigma\sqrt{2\pi}} \exp(-t^2/2\sigma^2) \leftrightarrow \exp(-2\pi^2 \sigma^2 f^2)$

And the transform of $d(t)$ becomes

$$d(t) \leftrightarrow \lim_{\sigma \to 0} \exp(-2\pi^2 \sigma^2 f^2) = 1 \quad \text{for } f < \infty$$

By a similar approach it can be shown that $x(t) = 1$ has the transform $d(f)$. Thus,

(A14)
$$d(t) \leftrightarrow 1$$
$$1 \leftrightarrow d(f)$$

Function $d(t)$ represents an infinitely narrow peak or impulse at the origin $t = 0$ of magnitude or effect equal to 1. A similar impulse at instant $t = t_o$ is expressed by $d(t-t_o)$. The following integral has useful properties.

$$\int_{-\infty}^{\infty} x(t) \, d(t-t_o) \, dt = \int_{-\infty}^{\infty} x(t+t_o) \, d(t) \, dt$$

Since the integrand on the right hand side is zero, except in the immediate neighborhood of the origin, the same integral dan be further developed

$$= \lim_{e \to 0} \int_{-e}^{+e} x(t+t_o) \, d(t) \, dt = x(t_o) \lim_{e \to 0} \int_{-e}^{+e} d(t) dt$$

The last integral is by (A11) equal to 1 and

(A15)
$$\int_{-\infty}^{+\infty} x(t) \, d(t-t_o) \, dt = x(t_o)$$

Expression (A15) is the convolution of $x(t)$ by $d(t-t_o)$ (see paragraph A4.).

A3. The Inverse Transform

The inverse operation of (A1) is denoted by F^{-1}

(A16) $\quad F^{-1}(X(f)) = x(t) = \int_{-\infty}^{\infty} X(f) \exp(2\pi i t f) \, df$

To prove (A16) we write heuristically

$$\int_{-\infty}^{\infty} X(f) \, e^{2\pi i f t} \, df = \int_{-\infty}^{\infty} \left[\int_{-\infty}^{\infty} x(z) e^{-2\pi i z f} dz \right] e^{2\pi i f t} df$$

$$= \int_{-\infty}^{\infty} \int_{-\infty}^{\infty} x(z) \, e^{-2\pi i (z-t) f} \, dz \, df$$

$$= \int_{-\infty}^{\infty} x(z) \left[\int_{-\infty}^{\infty} e^{-2\pi i (z-t) f} \, df \right] dz$$

The integral in brackets is by the second equation (A14) equal to $F(1)_{f=z-t} = d(z-t)$, and we continue

$$= \int_{-\infty}^{\infty} x(z) \, d(z-t) \, dz = x(t)$$

which proves (A16).

Notice that the inverse transform is the same operation as (A1) except for the sign in the exponent function.

It is readily shown that

(A17)
$$F^{-1}(x(t)) = X^{*}(f)$$
$$F^{-1}(x(-t)) = X(f)$$

It is seen from (A8) by reversing the sign of f that Re X(f) is even and Im X(f) is an odd function of f. By the same approach as on page A2 we see that

$$\text{(A18)} \quad x(t) = 2 \int_0^\infty \left[\text{Re } X(f)\right] \cos 2\pi t f \; df + 2 \int_0^\infty \left[\text{Im } X(f)\right] \sin 2\pi t f \; df$$

where the first term is $= x_e(t)$ and the second $= x_o(t)$.

By (A18) $x(t)$ is expressed as a superposition of cosine and sine waves of amplitudes Re X(f) and Im X(f) at frequencies f. Hence, function X(f) represents the (complex) <u>frequency spectrum</u> of the time function $x(t)$.

A4. The Convolution Integral

The convolution $v(t)$ of the two functions $x(t)$ and $y(t)$ is defined by the integral

$$\text{(A19)} \quad v(t) = \int_{-\infty}^{\infty} x(z) \, y(t-z) \, dz = \int_{-\infty}^{\infty} x(t-z) \, y(z) \, dz = x(t) \ast y(t)$$

where the operator $\ast$ between the function is a shorthand notation of the integral.

The first of the above integrals is illustrated in Fig. A1. where the element $x(z)dz$ of the first function takes the shape of y(t) reflected about the ordinate axis and shifted to z. v(t) is the superposition of all such elements.

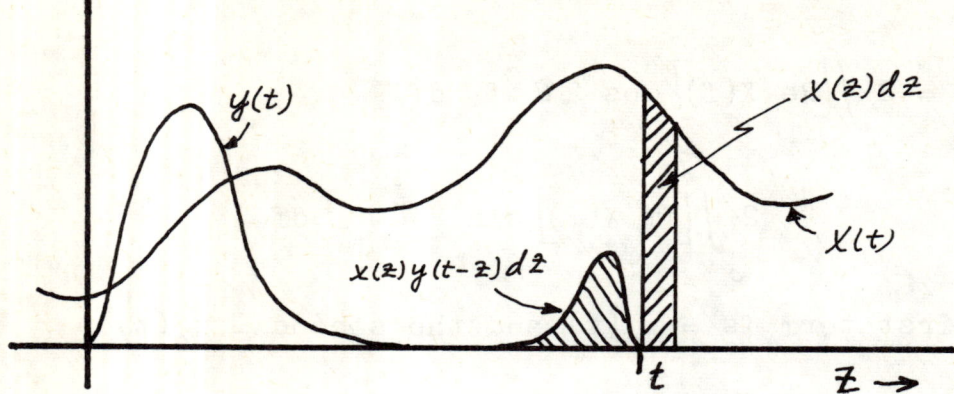

Fig. A1.

The convolution is a linear, commutative and associative operation

(A20) $\quad x(t) * y(t) = y(t) * x(t)$

(A21) $\quad x(t) * [h(t)+y(t)] = x(t) * h(t) + x(t) * y(t)$

(A22) $\quad x * (h * y) = (x * h) * y = x * h * y$

The Fourier transform of (A19) is

(A23) $\quad x(t) * y(t) \leftrightarrow V(f) = X(f) Y(f)$

That is, convolution in the time domain corresponds to multiplication of the transforms (frequency spectra). By symmetry we have also

(A24) $\quad x(t) y(t) \leftrightarrow X(f) * Y(f)$

To prove (A23) take the inverse transform of the product $X(f)Y(f)$.

$$X(f)Y(f) \leftrightarrow \int_{-\infty}^{\infty} X(f) \left[\int_{-\infty}^{\infty} y(z)e^{-2\pi i z f} dz\right] e^{2\pi i f t} df$$

$$= \int_{-\infty}^{\infty} y(z) \left[\int_{-\infty}^{\infty} X(f)e^{2\pi i f(t-z)} df\right] dz$$

$$= \int_{-\infty}^{\infty} y(z)x(t-z) dz = y(t) \star x(t)$$

$$= x(t) \star y(t)$$

We get by Equation (A4)

$$\int_{-\infty}^{\infty} x(t) \star y(t)\, dt = \left[X(f)Y(f)\right]_{f=0} = X(0)Y(0)$$

(A25)
$$= \int_{-\infty}^{\infty} x(t)dt \int_{-\infty}^{\infty} y(t)dt$$

That is, the integral of a convolution is equal to the product of the integrals of the component functions all taken over the whole time domain.

A special case of convolution

(A26) $\quad x(t) \star x(-t) \leftrightarrow X(f)X^*(f) = |X(f)|^2$

The square $|X(f)|^2$ of the absolute value of the frequency spectrum is called the **power spectrum** of $x(t)$ since the power of an electric signal is proportional to the square of the amplitude.

A5. Repetition and Comb

The following two operators are most useful when dealing with periodic and sampled signals (see P. M. Woodward). We define

$$\text{(A27)} \qquad \text{rep}_T \, x(t) = \sum_{k=-\infty}^{+\infty} x(t-kT)$$

$$\text{(A28)} \qquad \text{comb}_T \, x(t) = x(t) \sum_{k=-\infty}^{+\infty} d(t-kT)$$

$$= x(t) \, \text{rep}_T \, d(t)$$

The repetition of $x(t)$ to period T (A27) is obtained as the superposition of $x(t)$ when shifted by all multiples of the period T. See Fig. A2.

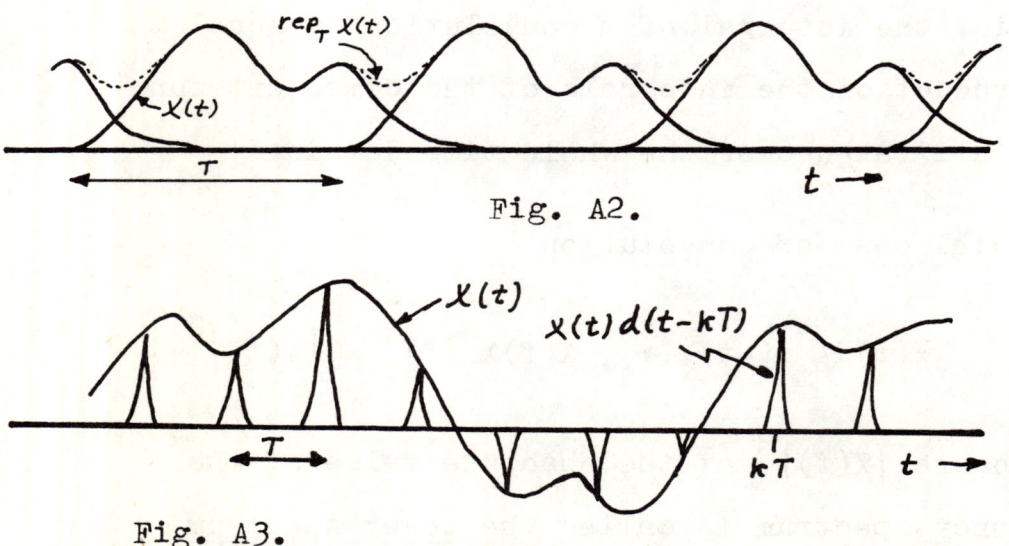

Fig. A2.

Fig. A3.

The comb operator is a sampler operator, where the signal x(t) is multiplied by an infinite equidistant (T) series of unit peak functions (delta functions) resembling the teeth of a comb. This operation is illustrated in Fig. A3.

By Equation (A15) we can, also, write

(A29) $\quad \text{rep}_T\, x(t) = x(t) * \text{rep}_T\, d(t)$

If we knew the transform of $\text{rep}_T\, d(t)$ we could write the transform of (A29) or (A27) as the product (A23) of the two transforms of the right hand side of (A29).

By using the definition (A1) and properties (A3), (A2), (A14) and definition (A27)

$$\text{rep}_T\, d(t) \leftrightarrow \sum_{k=-\infty}^{\infty} F(d(t-kT))$$

$$= \sum_{k=-\infty}^{\infty} \exp(-2\pi i T f)$$

To study the properties of this infinite series we take first a finite range of summation and then let it grow indefinitely. Take summation from -K to +K.

(A30) $\quad \displaystyle\sum_{k=-K}^{+K} \exp(-2\pi i T f) = \sin \pi K f T / \sin \pi f T$

(A30) is illustrated in Fig. A4. as function of f.

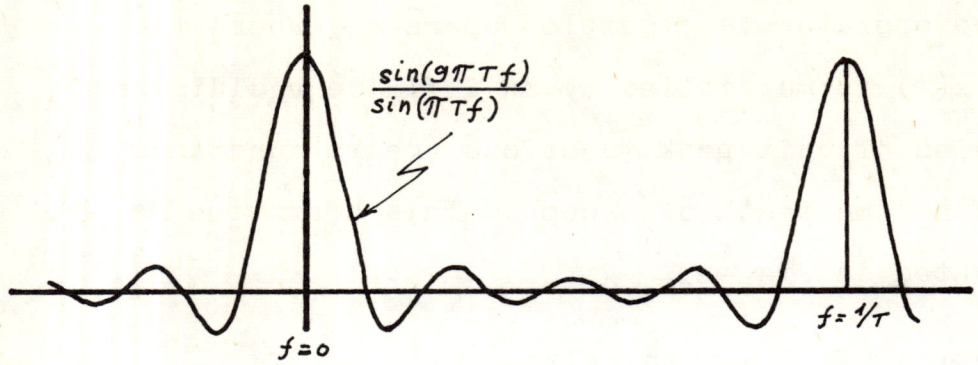

Fig. A4.

It can be shown that the integral of (A30) over one period $(-1/2T, +1/2T)$ is $1/T$ independently of K.

If we now let K grow indefinitely (A30) approaches zero at all other values of f except when $f = k/T$. At these points the function is equal to K and approaches infinity.

Obviously, then (A30) approaches

(A31) $\text{rep}_T \, d(t) \leftrightarrow \frac{1}{T} \text{rep}_{1/T} \, d(f)$

Thus,

(A32) $\text{rep}_T \, x(t) \leftrightarrow \frac{1}{T} X(f) * \text{rep}_{1/T} \, d(f)$
$= \frac{1}{T} \text{comb}_{1/T} \, X(f)$

Applying (A32) in reverse we get the transform of (A28).

(A33) $\text{comb}_T x(t) \leftrightarrow X(f) * \frac{1}{T} \text{rep}_{1/T} \, d(f)$
$= (1/T) \text{rep}_{1/T} \, X(f)$

Equations (A32) and (A33) can be interpreted: A periodic time function generated by the repetition has a discrete frequency spectrum at harmonic frequences k/T. The discrete time function $\text{comb}_t\, x(t)$ generated by sampling $x(t)$ at intervals T has a periodic frequency spectrum obtained by repeating the spectrum of the continuous signal to period $1/T$.

A6. Fourier Series

The repetition of a nonperiodic function $x(t)$ is periodic. Conversely, every periodic function, say, $y(t)$ can be expressed as a repetition of some nonperiodic function. The number of possible functions giving $y(t)$ by the repetition is infinite. The simplest among these, perhaps, is the one that is equal to $y(t)$ over just one period and zero outside.

Let us denote by $q(t)$ a function such that

$$(A34) \qquad q(t) = \begin{cases} y(t) & \text{when } -\tfrac{1}{2}T < t \leq \tfrac{1}{2}T \\ 0 & \text{elsewhere} \end{cases}$$

assuming that the period of $y(t)$ is T.

Then
$$(A35) \qquad y(t) = \text{rep}_T\, q(t)$$

and
$$(A36) \qquad Y(f) = \frac{1}{T} \text{comb}_{1/T}\, Q(f) = \frac{Q(f)}{T} \sum_{k=-\infty}^{\infty} d(f-k/T)$$

That is, the transform of a periodic time function $y(t)$ with a period T consists of a set of delta functions at regular intervals $1/T$ in the frequency domain.

Let us denote the "weight" of the kth peak by A_k

(A37) $$A_k = \frac{Q(k/T)}{T}$$

Hence (A36) becomes

(A38) $$Y(f) = \sum_{k=-\infty}^{\infty} A_k \, d(f-k/T)$$

The inverse of (A38) gives the Fourier series expression of $y(t)$

(A39) $$y(t) = \sum_{k=-\infty}^{\infty} A_k \exp(2\pi i k t/T)$$

This is the complex form of the Fourier series. By (A8) we get the cosine and sine coefficients a_k and b_k using also (A34) and (A37)

(A40)
$$a_k = \frac{2}{T} \int_0^{T/2} y_e(t) \cos 2\pi k t/T \, dt$$
$$b_k = -\frac{2}{T} \int_0^{T/2} y_o(t) \sin 2\pi k t/T \, dt$$

where y_e and y_o are the even and odd components of $y(t)$. By substituting $A_k = a_k + i b_k$ to (A39) and since $a_{-k} = a_k$ and $b_{-k} = -b_k$ we get the standard Fourier series expression

$$(A41) \quad y(t) = a_o + 2\sum_{k=1} a_k \cos 2\pi kt/T$$

$$- 2\sum_{k=1} b_k \sin 2\pi kt/T$$

Notice that if the sign of b_k in (A40) is defined +, the second summation in (A41) has also sign +. The summation is started at $k = 1$ since always $b_o = 0$.

A7. Truncation

Assume that we neglect (or do not know) all the frequencies higher than a given limiting frequency $f = w$. What will be the effect of this on the time variable $y(t)$ in (A41) or $x(t)$ in (A18)?

We can represent this truncation of the transform by multiplication of the transform by the **rectangular** function defined by

$$(A42) \quad \mathrm{rect}(f) = \begin{cases} 1 & \text{when} \quad -\tfrac{1}{2} < f \leq +\tfrac{1}{2} \\ 0 & \text{elsewhere} \end{cases}$$

This has the transform

$$(A43) \quad \mathrm{rect}(f) \leftrightarrow \sin(\pi t)/\pi t = \mathrm{sinc}(t)$$

where the function $\mathrm{sinc}(t)$ is defined by (A43).

Due to symmetry we have also

(A44) $\text{sinc}(t) \leftrightarrow \text{rect}(f)$

The truncated spectrum can be now written

(A45) $X_t(f) = X(f)\, \text{rect}(f/2w)$

and the time variable $x_t(t)$ from the truncated spectrum (A45) is

(A45) $x_t(t) = x(t) * 2w\, \text{sinc}(2wt)$

$\qquad\qquad = x(t) * \dfrac{\sin(2\pi wt)}{t}$

Sinc(t) has the properties

(A46) $\displaystyle\int_{-\infty}^{\infty} \text{sinc}(t)\, dt = 1$

$\qquad\qquad \text{sinc}(0) = 1$

And has the general shape given in Fig. A5.

With high values of w
$2w\, \text{sinc}(2wt)$ approaches
the delta function $d(t)$.
A finite w gives a
smoothing effect on $x_t(t)$
in (A45)

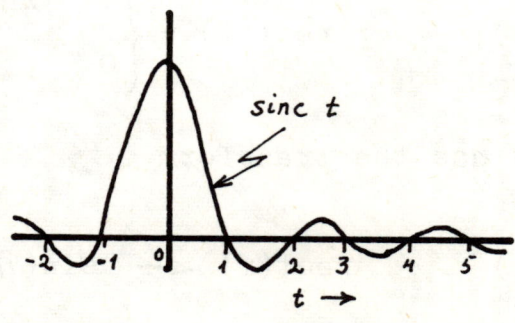

Fig. A5.

A8. Numerical Fourier Transforms

A numerical algorithm of the Fourier transform can be based on equations (A8).

Let us assume, first, that the function $x(t)$ is band limited by frequency w, and that the even and odd components of $x(t)$ vanish outside the interval $(-T, +T)$. (Strictly, these two conditions are never met simultaneously.)

In this case the integral is replaced by the sampled form

$$(A47) \quad \operatorname{Re} X(f) = \Delta t \sum_k x_e(k \Delta t) \cos 2\pi k \Delta t f$$

where $\Delta t \leqslant 1/2w$ is the sampling interval and the range of summation is from $-n = -T/\Delta t$ to $+n = T/\Delta t$.

Since the time variable function $x(t)$ is limited by range T the transform $X(f)$ is fully determined by samples at intervals $1/2T$ (Sampling theorem applied to inverse transform).

Let us adopt further notations

$$(A48) \quad \begin{aligned} x_{ek} &= 2x_e(k\Delta t)\Delta t \\ x_{ok} &= 2x_o(k\Delta t)\Delta t \\ f &= j\Delta f = j/2T \\ C_{kj} &= \cos(\pi k j/n) \\ S_{kj} &= \sin(\pi k j/n) \end{aligned}$$

Expression (A47) and the associated imaginary component can be written with this notation

(A49)
$$\text{Re } X(j/2T) = \tfrac{1}{2}x_{eo} + \sum_{k=1}^{n} x_{ek} C_{kj}$$
$$\text{Im } X(j/2T) = - \sum_{k=1}^{n} x_{ok} S_{kj}$$

The summations in (A49) are recognized as an n by n matrix multiplication by an n-vector. But matrices C_{kj} and S_{kj} can be also considered as cyclic one-dimensional arrays of cycle n. The jth row of the matrix is composed of every j^{th} element of this array.

The continuous form of (A49) can be constructed by applying the sinc-interpolation (81).

We get by the same approach the inverse transform

(A50)
$$x_e(k/2w) = \tfrac{1}{2} X_{Ro} + \sum_{j=1}^{n} X_{Rj} C_{kj}$$
$$x_o(k/2w) = \sum_{j=1}^{n} X_{Ij} S_{kj}$$

where
$$X_{Rj} = 2 \Delta f \text{ Re } X(j \Delta f)$$
$$X_{Ij} = 2 \Delta f \text{ Im } X(j \Delta f)$$

By replacing the integral (A8) by the summation (A47) we are, in effect, computing the transform

(A51) $\quad \Delta t \text{ comb}_{\Delta t} x(t) \leftrightarrow \text{rep}_{1/\Delta t} X(f)$

The interval of repetition in (A51) is $1/\Delta t = n/T = 2n\Delta f$. If the sampling interval Δt in (A47) is longer than required by the sampling theorem, $\Delta t > 1/2w$, that is, $w > 1/2\Delta t$, the successive repetitions of $X(f)$ overlap to certain extent in the range 0 to $n\Delta f$. This effect is illustrated in Fig. A6.

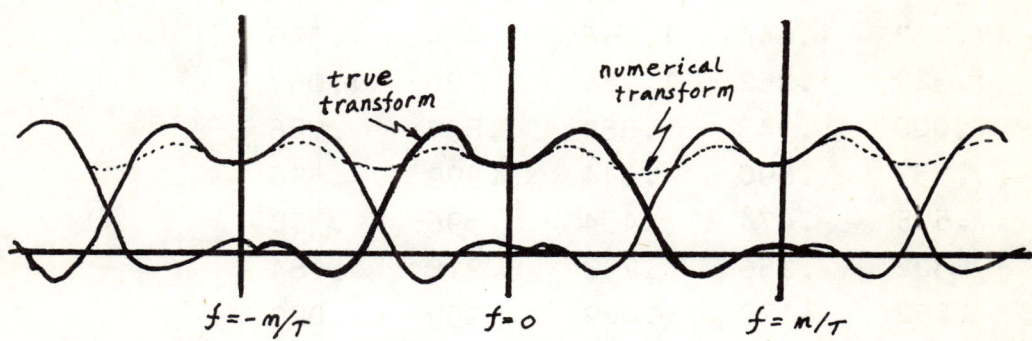

Fig. A6.

For the same reason, with 2n samples of $x(t)$ at intervals Δt it is impossible to compute spectrum $X(f)$ beyond the frequency $j = n$ or $f = 1/2\Delta t$. If j is made to exceed n in (A49) we get only repetitions or "ghosts" of the true spectrum.

For computer programs of Fourier transform see, for example, IBM System/360 Scientific Subroutine Package, (360A-CM-03X) IBM Manual H20-0205.

The method is described in more detail in the IBM Research Paper RC 1743, J. W. Cooley, P. A. W. Lewis, P. D. Welch, "The Fast Fourier Transform Algorithm and its Applications". (1967).

APPENDIX B

BINARY LOGARITHMS AND ENTROPIES

p	.00	.02	.04	.06	.08
.0	∞	5.644	4.644	4.059	3.644
.1	3.322	3.059	2.837	2.644	2.474
.2	2.322	2.184	2.059	1.943	1.837
.3	1.737	1.644	1.556	1.474	1.396
.4	1.322	1.252	1.184	1.120	1.059
.5	1.000	.943	.889	.837	.786
.6	.737	.690	.644	.599	.556
.7	.515	.474	.434	.396	.358
.8	.322	.286	.252	.218	.184
.9	.152	.120	.089	.059	.029

Table B1. $-\log_2 p$

p	.00	.02	.04	.06	.08
.0	.0000	.1129	.1858	.2435	.2915
.1	.3322	.3671	.3971	.4230	.4453
.2	.4644	.4806	.4941	.5053	.5142
.3	.5211	.5260	.5292	.5306	.5305
.4	.5288	.5256	.5211	.5153	.5083
.5	.5000	.4906	.4800	.4684	.4558
.6	.4422	.4276	.4121	.3956	.3783
.7	.3602	.3412	.3215	.3009	.2796
.8	.2575	.2348	.2113	.1871	.1623
.9	.1368	.1107	.0839	.0565	.0286

Table B2. $-p \log_2 p$

APPENDIX C

PROBLEMS

1. A motor vehicle licence plate numbering system utilizes a code with three letters followed by three digits, for example, KST 573. What is the information capacity of a plate (expressed in bits)?

   What is this capacity if all 6 positions may be alphanumeric (a letter or a digit) assuming an alphabet of 26 letters?

   What is the minimum length m′ (see (10)) in the latter coding system for 150 000 vehicles?

2. Derive by the definition (17) the entropy of the geometric distribution

$$p_j = \begin{cases} (1-e^{-\lambda}) e^{-\lambda j} & j \geq 0 \\ 0 & j < 0 \end{cases}$$

   Hint:
$$\sum_{j=0}^{\infty} j\, x^{-j} = x/(x-1)^2 \qquad x > 1$$

3. Find the numerical value of entropy for the distribution

j	1	2	3	4	5	6	7
p_j	.17	.25	.28	.12	.09	.06	.03

   $p_j = 0$ for all other j.

4. There are 12 coins, identical in appearance, in a box. It is known that one of them is a counterfeit of different weight, but it is not known whether it is heavier or lighter than the genuine coins.

You have a balancing scale with three possible indications: left cup down, balanced, right cup down. How can you identify the counterfeit coin in three weighings and tell if it is heavier or lighter?

Give this classical quiz an information theoretical treatment in the form of a three level (number of weighings) ternary (three possible outcomes) decision tree.

Show that the information in the three weighings equals the initial entropy (ignorance).

5. The popular party game "20 questions" is played as follows. A persons name is chosen unbeknownst to you. You have to identify the person (a personal aquaintance or a celebrity) by means of questions that are answered "yes" or "no". The maximum number of questions allowed is 20.

This process can be represented by a binary decisio tree of maximum 20 levels. A maximum information (one bit) per question is gained if the à priori probabilities of the two answers are equal.

What is the maximum number of the "population" of persons out of which you can identify the chosen name with certainty? What is your strategy?

(Normally the game is played so that a subset of the population is defined by one or more common properties. Assume that this can be done also by enumeration, which, however, would make the game extremely dull.)

6. Assume, further, in the above game that the population is infinite, but you know from a long experience of play that the person is chosen with a geometric à priori distribution (see Problem 2.). What are your best chances of success with a parameter λ?

If questions can be continued beyond 20, what is the smallest λ that would still make it possible to keep the mean number of questions per game below 20?

7. Assume that the international Morse code (1837) composed of dots (.) and dashes (-) has the following durations of its elements in suitable time units (bit times).
dot = 1 unit, dash = 3 units, space between dots and dashes within a letter code = 1 unit, space between consecutive letters in a word = 3 units,

word space = letter space + 3 = 6 units.

letter	code	t	letter	code	t
word space		3	N	-.	8
A	.-	8	O	---	14
B	-...	12	P	.--.	14
C	-.-.	14	Q	--.-	16
D	-..	10	R	.-.	10
E	.	4	S	...	8
F	..-.	12	T	-	6
G	--.	12	U	..-	10
H	....	8	V	...-	12
I	..	6	W	.--	12
J	.---	16	X	-..-	14
K	-.-	12	Y	-.--	16
L	.-..	12	Z	--..	14
M	--	10			

Table C1.

Table C1. gives the codes and respective durations t. Using the letter frequencies of Table 6. or Table 7. compute the mean information rate per code and per bit time in English or German assuming independence of successive letters. Compute the coding efficiency (35).

Study if the coding efficiency could be improved by reassignment of the same codes to the alphabets, that is, by rearrangement of the column "code" in Table C1. What is the improved efficiency?

8. Design a variable length binary code for the case of Table 1. which has a higher coding efficiency than the code given in the same table.

9. Design a variable length binary code for the alphabets of independent probabilities of Table 6. or Table 7. with as high coding efficiency as possible (optimum code) by assigning code words to single letters.

10. Design an optimum code for the case of Table 1. by the Shannon-Fano method starting from the original binary character set with $p_1 = 1/6$, $p_2 = 5/6$. In how many steps can you reach the same efficiency as in Problem 8?

11. An artificial language has the following properties.
    - The language has a 27 character alphabet, same as Table 6.
    - The first letter of a word has a uniform distribution ($p = 1/26$) over all letters.
    - A consonant is always followed by a vowel (a,e,i,o,u,y) also with uniform probability, or a word space (see below).
    - A vowel is always followed by a consonant with uniform probability distribution, or a word space.
    - A word space is always followed by a letter (first letter of a word). The probability of a word space

(end of word) is constant = 1/5 after all letters.

Show that the word length distribution is geometric (see Problem 2.).

Write the conditional probability matrix $p_i(j)$ of character S_j following character S_i (see page 58). Compute $p_i(39)$, the single character probability distribution.
Compute the unconditional information $I(i)$ and the conditional information $I_i(j)$ by (43) and (49). What is the mean information rate per character and the redundancy of this language?

12. Shannon has suggested the following two person game for obtaining an upper bound of the information rate of a natural language.
    - The first player selects a representative text from a newspaper or a book unknown to the second player.
    - The second player has to construct the text by means of questions that are answered "yes" or "no". (Compare with the game "20 questions" in Problem 5.)
    - The maximum information that can be gained equals the number of questions. Hence, the information rate per letter is equal to or less than the number of questions divided by the number of characters (letters and spaces) in the text.

No limits are imposed on the questions. They may be constructed to define an enumerated set of characters, (Is the next character one of the following: A, C, F, I, or "space"?) or a sequence of characters (Are the next three letters "ATE " or "ING "?), or full words (Are the next two words "INFORMATION THEORY"?).

In order to eliminate the "transient" effect the first player should start by reading out a couple of sentences.

This game is suggested to the students as an educational passtime.

If a time-sharing computer and terminal is available it is suggested that the computer is programmed in the role of the first player.

13. Write a program to produce matrix $p_i(j)$ for a natural language. Use as input, say, 10 000 character text (125 full punched cards).

14. Table C2. gives the channel matrix of a very noisy channel of character set (n=4) A,B,C,D.

i	j	1	2	3	4	p_i
A	1	.35	.20	.30	.15	.10
B	2	.60	.20	.10	.10	.40
C	3	.30	.50	.10	.10	.40
D	4	.45	.10	.10	.35	.10

Table C2.

Find the information rate I of this channel using Equation (62).

Verify that I is constant with respect to permutation of the columns of $p_i(j)$. Thus, the permutation $j = 3,1,2,4$ interpreted at the receiver as sequence A,B,C,D has the same I. This would be the natural interpretation since most of the diagonal elements $p_i(i)$ are the highest probabilities (but not all).

The reason why I is invariant with the permutation is that the assignment of character values to the received codes is a semantic process not included in the syntactic theory.

15. Consider a fixed length three bit binary code ($n = 2^3 = 8$) (non-redundant). Assume that bit errors are independent with probability $p = .1$. Write the channel matrix $p_i(j)$ and compute the information rate when $p_i = 1/8$ for all i.

16. Find the channel capacity and the respective à priori distribution p_i for the ideal observer whose à posteriori (inverse conditional) probabilities $p_k(i)$ are given in Table 23.

17. Consider a binary channel with independent bit errors of constant probability $p = .001$. A parity check (first order error checking) code will be

used. It is required that the mean number of undetected errors does not exceed one code word out of 100 000. Which is the longest code word length m that can be used? What is the relative frequency of code words with a detected error?

18. Assume that in the channel of Problem 17. we are using the highest acceptable code word length m in the parity checking code. A long message is divided into blocks of length mk bits, each containing k code words (no LRC character). If no errors are detected in a block the transmission of the next block is started. One or more errors found in the block initiate a retransmission of the whole block.

    Assume that the acknowledgement and request for retransmission take a turnaround time equal to two code word times (2m bit times).

    Find the block length that maximizes the effective information rate. What is this rate?

    Compute the channel capacity (symmetric channel) and verify that the effective information rate does not exceed the capacity.

    Hint: Entropy of the binomial distribution (69) can be written
    $$H = -\sum_i \left[\binom{m}{i} p^i (1-p)^{m-i} \log\binom{m}{i}\right] - m(p\log p + (1-p)\log(1-p))$$

When $mp \ll 1$ only the term $i=1$ of the summation is significant and the expression becomes approximately

$$H = mp \log\left(\frac{e}{mp}\right) \quad \text{(show this)}$$

19. The ten visual patterns below represent decimal digits from 0 to 9. They utilize a two-dimensional field of four by six bits (24 bits).

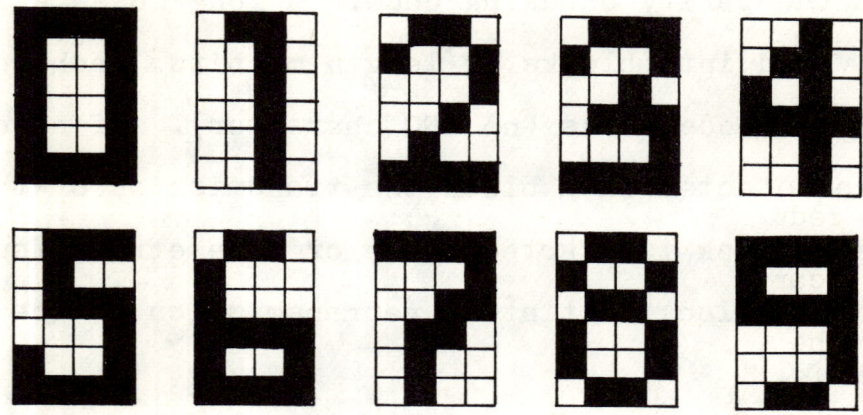

What is the redundancy of this code?
Write the distance matrix d_{ij} giving the number of different bit states in digits i and j. What is the minimum distance?

A received pattern k is interpreted as i having the smallest distance d_{ik} to k. If more than one, say, i and j of the above patterns are at the same smallest distance from k ($d_{ik} = d_{jk}$) this generates an error condition.

How do you interpret the two patterns on the next page?

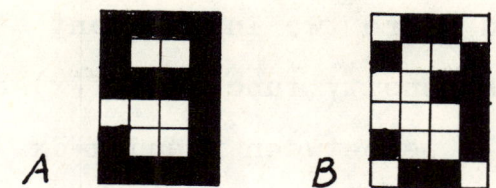

A   B

Can you design another set of ten visual patterns (not necessarily based on the digits) with a higher minimum distance using the same four by six bit field?

What is the highest possible order of error correction according to the Hamming Bound (75)?

20. A redundancy code with a minimum Hamming distance = 3 can be used either as an error correcting code of the first order or a error detecting code of the second order. Which factors should be considered when deciding between these two possible uses?

21. Show that the first order error correcting code $m = 3$, $c = 2$, $t = 1$, (Fig. 16) is equivalent to a majority vote in a threefold repetition.

What is the difference in error correction between this code and transmitting a long message three times in succession without redundancy? (repetition on bit level versus repetition on message level) Is it immaterial, from the point of view of error correction, which of the two opposing vertices of cube in Fig. 16. are chosen?

22. Show that if x and y are two independent statistical variables with density functions $f(x)$ and $g(y)$ (probability that x is between x and x+dx is $f(x)dx$) the density function of the sum $t = x + y$ is the convolution $h(t) = f(t) * g(t)$ where $h(t)$ is the density function of t.

23. Show using the convolution theorem of Problem 22. that under the mentioned conditions the means and variances are additive for arbitrary distributions.

$$\bar{t} = \bar{x} + \bar{y}$$

$$\text{var}(t) = \text{var}(x) + \text{var}(y)$$

24. Discuss a continuous band limited channel (limit frequency w) in which the amplitude of $x(t)$ is limited to range $(-A, +A)$. Assume that $x(t)$ is uniformly distributed between these limits

$$p(x) = \frac{1}{2A} \text{rect}(x/2A)$$

Assume also that the samples u_k of the noise $u(t)$ are similarly distributed and limited by the amplitude in range $(-a, +a)$ so that successive u_k are stationary and independent.

Use (62) in the continuous form $I = H(y) - H_x(y)$ with

$$H(y) = -\int_{-\infty}^{\infty} p(y) \log p(y) \, dy$$

$$H_x(y) = - \int_{-\infty}^{\infty} p(x) \int_{-\infty}^{\infty} p_x(y) \log p_x(y) \, dy \, dx$$

to show that the information rate is

$$I = \begin{cases} 2w \log(A/a) + \dfrac{aw}{A} \log e & ; \ a \leq A \\ \dfrac{Aw}{a} \log e & ; \ a \geq A \end{cases}$$

Hint: Use the convolution theorem of Problem 22. to compute $p(y)$.

Is the above information rate at the same time the capacity of the channel or is there some other $p(x)$ that would give a higher rate?

25. A quantity x is known in advance to be normally distributed about a mean $\bar{x}$ with a variance $\sigma^2 = 100$. The value is computed accurately but the result is given as the nearest integer. What is the mean of the gained information?

Use the form $I = H(x) - H_y(x)$ where $H_y(x)$ is a mixture of a continuous and discrete case

$$H_y(x) = - \sum_j p(j) \int_{-\infty}^{\infty} p_y(x) \log p_y(x) \, dx$$

26. Repeat Problem 25. for the case that $p(x)$ is uniformly distributed in range $(0, 10^n)$.

27. Reconsider the detection of two possible levels $x = 0$ and $x = 1$ in Gaussian noise (see pages 132 to 134). Assume, now, that the two kinds of errors, 0 received as 1 = first kind (probability p_q) and 1 received as 0 = second kind (probability p_r), do not have equally grave consequences. Denote the respective penalties C_q and C_r. How should we determine the level of discrimination $\bar{y}_k$ to minimize the mean rate of penalties?

    Give the numerical value for case $p_o = 4/5$, $p_1 = 1/5$, $R = 3$, and $C_r/C_q = 2$.

28. Can you define an ideal observer for the channel defined in Problem 24?

    Describe the ideal observer for the same case with the assumption that $p(x)$ is a normal distribution with zero mean and variance σ_x^2 but same noise as in Problem 24.

29. Show that the signal to noise ratio for a set of wave forms $x_i(t)$ of equal mean energies and durations of m sample intervals $T = m/2w$ is

$$R = P_x/P_N = c_{ii}/m\sigma_N^2$$

    where

$$c_{ii} = \sum_k{}' x_{ik}^2$$

    Assume a Gaussian noise with variance σ_N^2.

30. Try to find another set of three wave forms $x_i(t)$, defined by 5 samples such as those in Table 29. but with higher mutual (minimum) distances d_{ij} than those in Table 33. computed for the set of Table 29. Assume that all $p_i = 1/3$ and the mean energy is constrained by $c_{ii} = 3$.

    Obviously such a set would generate a lower error rate with the same signal to noise ratio R.

31. The integral of the absolute value of expression (153)

    $$X_{ij} = \int_{-\infty}^{\infty} |X_i(f) X_j(f)| \, df$$

    when normalized by $X_{ii} = c_{ii}$

    $$\bar{X}_{ij} = X_{ij}/X_{ii}$$

    can be used as a measure for the suitability of the set of wave forms $x_i(t)$ for an unsynchronous reception. If condition (153) is satisfied $\bar{X}_{ij}$ is the identity matrix with $\bar{X}_{ii} = 1$ and $\bar{X}_{ij} = 0$ for $i \neq j$. Non-zero elements off the diagonal indicate a degree of interference between corresponding wave forms.

    Develop matrix $\bar{X}_{ij}$ for the wave forms in Table 29. or those found in Problem 30. to see how well they could be used for unsynchronous transmission.

32. Radioactive tracers are used in a hydraulic system to determine time delays in the flow between some critical points. It is known by theoretical considerations that a small amount of tracer solution injected in the stream will be spread out due to mixing at the point of detection into a pulse of form $x(t)$

$$x(t) = \begin{cases} b(t-t_o) \exp(-a(t-t_o)) & t > t_o \\ 0 & t \leq t_o \end{cases}$$

where t is the time measured from the moment of injection and t_o is the moment when the first effects of the tracer are expected at the point of observation.

The signal $x(t)$ is superimposed by Gaussian noise due to the background radiation of natural radioactivity and cosmic radiation.

Design an off-line numerical filter for the determination of the delay t_o. What do you consider as a sufficiently short sampling interval in terms of a?

Table C3. gives a series of measurements done over a period of 50 minutes at intervals of 1 minute. It is known that at this point $1/a$ is about 3 minutes and that t_o is with certainty between 5 and 45 minutes.

t	y(t)	t	y(t)	t	y(t)	t	y(t)	t	y(t)
1	232	11	206	21	228	31	217	41	184
2	147	12	150	22	217	32	208	42	242
3	230	13	113	23	221	33	212	43	174
4	245	14	239	24	262	34	128	44	215
5	147	15	215	25	227	35	250	45	218
6	237	16	243	26	259	36	216	46	254
7	275	17	261	27	258	37	229	47	256
8	286	18	228	28	203	38	169	48	265
9	200	19	286	29	264	39	94	49	228
10	124	20	266	30	186	40	207	50	112

Table C3.

It is known, also, that the mean level of the background radiation is 200 with a variance of $\sigma_N^2 = 830$. The amplitude of the signal (b) is not known.

What is the ratio of the probabilities of the most probable t_o and the next probable delay?

33. Prove the so called Parseval's Theorem

$$\int_{-\infty}^{\infty} x(t)y(t)dt = \int_{-\infty}^{\infty} X(f)Y(-f)df = \int_{-\infty}^{\infty} X(-f)Y(f)df$$

for arbitrary (real) functions $x(t)$ and $y(t)$.

34. Prove equation

$$\int_{-\infty}^{\infty} \text{sinc}(x-m)\text{sinc}(x-n)dx = \begin{cases} 1 & ; m=n \\ 0 & ; m \neq n \end{cases}$$

INDEX

A

Analog filter, 163

B

Band pass filter, 152
Band width, 107
Binomial distribution, 89
Bit, 17
Bit errors, 89
Burst errors, 103

C

Capacity
    Continuous channel, 119
    Noisy channel, 77
Channel, 13
    Capacity, 15
    Continuous, 105, 119
    Discrete, 13
    Noiseless, 12, 25
Channel matrix, 73, 124
Channels in tandem, 86
Character, 7
    Valid, invalid, 88
Character set, 12
Check bit, 91
Code
    Cyclic, 103
    Error checking, 88

Code
    Error correcting, 88, 94
    First order correcting, 95
    Instantaneous, 48
    k-nary optimum, 40
    k-out-of-m, 101
    Morse, C3
    Non-instantaneous, 50
    Optimum, 35, 39
    Parity, 91
    Reversible, 49
    Uniquely decipherable, 48
    Variable length, 33
    2-out-of-5, 101
    4-out-of-8, 102
Code space, 90
Coding, 25
Coding efficiency, 29, 39
Comb, A9
Context, 4
Continuous signal, 105
    Band limited, 107
    Detection of, 124
    Ideal observer, 128
    Interpolation, 111
    Sampling, 107
Control characters, 47
Convolution, A6
    Filter, 145
    Reception, 154
    Square, 149
    Theorem, C12
Correlation reception, 134
Cosine-transform, A2
Criterion of detection, 143, 154
Cross correlation, 139
Cyclic code, 103

D

Decision tree
Delay in real-time filter, 160
Delta function, A3
Desampling, 107
Detection, criterion of, 143
Detection theory, 124
Deterministic observer, 86
Dirac's delta, A3
Distance, 140
    Hamming, 90
    In correlation detection, 138
Distribution
    Binomial, 89
    Exponential, 118
    Geometric, C1
    Normal, 126
Duration, 13

E

End of message condition, 45
Entropy, 21
    Binomial distribution, C9
    Continuous channel, 115
    Continuous distributions, 118
    Exponential distribution, 118
    Normal distribution, 118
    Discrete distribution, 22
Error checking, 10, 88
    First order, 90
    Hierarchy, 92
    Parity, 91
    Redundancy, 92
    Variable length code, 104

Error correcting, 88, 94
Euler's formula, A2
Even component, A2
Exponential smoothing, 160

F

Filter, 145
    Analog, 163
    Band pass, 152
    Low pass, 158
    Numerical, 157
    Off-line, 154
    Real-time, 154
Filter function, 150
Flag bit, 47
Floating average, 159
Fourier series, A12
Fourier transform, A1
    Numerical, A16
Frequency spectrum, A6
    Discrete, A12
    Periodic, A12
Fundamental theorem of information theory, 97, 123

G

Gaussian distribution, A3
Gaussian noise, 112
Geometric distribution, C1
Guesswork, 84

H

Hamming Bound, 100
Hamming distance, 90
Huffman code, 45

I

Ideal observer, 82, 87, 128
Information
    Capacity, 16
    Cell, 105, 8
    Conditional, 56
    Content, 17
    Continuous, 8, 115
    Discrete, 8
    Filter, 11, 145
    Rate, 20, 25
Information rate, 25
    Conditional, 62
    Noiseless channel, 22
    Noisy continuous channel, 119
    Noisy discrete channel, 75
    per letter, 64
Interpolation, 111
Invalid character, 83
Inverse Fourier transform, A5

J, K

Joint events, 51
Joint probability, 53, 59
k-out-of-m code

L

Letter frequencies, English, German, 52
Level of information, 2
Likelihood function, 124
Likelihood matrix, 73
Longitudinal redundancy check, 93
Low pass filter, 158
LRC, 93

M

Meaning, 1
Morse code, C3

N

Natural languages, 64
    Information rate, 71
    Word length, 69
    Word probabilities, 69
Noise, 14, 72
    Filtered, 150
    Gaussian, 112
    Power, of, 114, 158
    White, 112
Noisy channel, 72
    Capacity of, 77
    Ideal observer, 82
    Information rate, 75
    Symmetric, 77
    Unsymmetric, 79
Normal distribution, A3
Numerical filters, 157
Numerical Fourier transform, A16

O

Odd component, A2
Optimum codes, 35
    Huffman code, 45
    Natural language, 65
    Shannon-Fano method, 44

P

Parallel transmission, 57
Parity error checking, 91
Parseval's theorem, C17
Power spectrum, A8
Pragmatics, 4
Prediction, 6
Probability
    à posteriori, 74
    à priori, 73
    Conditional, 60
    Joint, 53

R

Real-time, 6
Record mark, 47
Rect-function, A14
Redundancy, 68
    Error checking, 92
    In time series, 157
Redundancy codes, 101
Repetition, A9
Response time, 6

S

Sampling, 107
Sampling theorem, 111
Semantics, 3
Serial transmission, 56
Shannon-Fano method, 44
Signal space, 139
Signal to noise ratio, C14, 122
Signal vector, 109, 139

Sinc-function, A14
Sinc-interpolation, 111
Sine-transform, A2
Smoothing, 155
Spectrum vector, 109
Statistical constraints, 67
Symmetric channel, 77
Synchronous transmission, 145
Syntactics, 2

T

Time series, 155
    Redundant, 157
Truncation, A14

U

Uncertainty, 1, 24
Unit peak function, A3
Unsymmetric channel, 79

V, W

Value, 2, 4
White noise, 112

Z

Zipf's law, 70

Offsetdruck: Julius Beltz, Weinheim/Bergstr.

Lecture Notes in Operations Research and Mathematical Economics

Vol. 1: H. Bühlmann, H. Loeffel, E. Nievergelt, Einführung in die Theorie und Praxis der Entscheidung bei Unsicherheit. IV, 125 Seiten 4°. 1967. DM 12,– / US $ 3.00

Vol. 2: U. N. Bhat, A Study of the Queueing Systems M/G/1 and GI/M/1. VIII, 78 pages 4°. 1968. DM 8,80 / US $ 2.20

Vol. 3: A. Strauss, An Introduction to Optimal Control Theory. VI, 153 pages. 4°. 1968. DM 14,– / US $ 3.50

Vol. 4 Einführung in die Methode Branch and Bound. Herausgegeben von F. Weinberg. VIII, 159 Seiten. 4°. 1968. DM 14,– / US $ 3.50

Ökonometrie und Unternehmensforschung
Econometrics and Operations Research

Herausgegeben von / Edited by

M. Beckmann, Bonn; R. Henn, Karlsruhe; A. Jaeger, Cincinnati; W. Krelle, Bonn; H. P. Künzi, Zürich; K. Wenke, Ludwigshafen; Ph. Wolfe, Santa Monica (Cal.)
Geschäftsführende Herausgeber / Managing Editors
W. Krelle und H. P. Künzi

Vol. I: Nichtlineare Programmierung. Von Hans Paul Künzi, Professor an der Universität Zürich und Wilhelm Krelle, Professor an der Universität Bonn. Unter Mitwirkung von Werner Oettli, Wissenschaftlicher Mitarbeiter, Wirtschaftswiss. Institut der Universität Zürich.
Mit 18 Abbildungen. XVI, 221 Seiten Gr.-8°. 1962. Ganzleinen DM 38,– ; US $ 9.50

Vol. II: Lineare Programmierung und Erweiterungen. Von George B. Dantzig, Chairman of the Operations Research Center and Professor of Operations Research, University of California, Berkeley.
Ins Deutsche übertragen und bearbeitet von Arno Jaeger, University of Cincinnati.
Mit 103 Abbildungen. XVI, 712 Seiten Gr.-8°. 1966. Ganzleinen DM 68,– ; US $ 17.00

Vol. III: Stochastic Processes. By M. Girault, Professor at the University of Paris.
With 35 figures. XII, 126 pages 8vo. 1966. Cloth DM 28,–; US $ 7.00

Vol. IV: Methoden der Unternehmensforschung im Versicherungswesen. Von Karl-H. Wolff, Dr. phil., Professor an der Technischen Hochschule Wien.
Mit 14 Diagrammen. VIII, 266 Seiten Gr.-8°. 1966. Ganzleinen DM 49,– ; US $ 12.25

Vol. V: The Theory of Max-Min and its Application to Weapons Allocation Problems. By John M. Danskin, Center for Naval Analyses of the Franklin-Institute, Arlington (Virginia).
With 6 figures. X, 126 pages 8vo. 1967. Cloth DM 32,–; US $ 8.00

Vol. VI: Entscheidungskriterien bei Risiko. Von Hans Schneeweiß, Professor am Institut für Ökonometrie der Universität des Saarlandes, Saarbrücken.
Mit 35 Abbildungen. XII, 214 Seiten Gr.-8°. 1967. Ganzleinen DM 48,– ; US $ 12.00

Vol. VII: Boolean Methods in Operations Research and Related Areas. By Peter L. Hammer (Ivănescu), Professor at the Technion-Israel Institute of Technology, Haifa, and Sergiu Rudeanu, Professor at the Academy of S. R. Roumania, Bucharest.
With 25 figures. XVI, 332 pages 8vo. 1968. Cloth DM 46,–; US $ 11.50

Vol. VIII: Strategy for R & D: Studies in the Microeconomics of Development. By Thomas Marschak, University of California, Berkeley, Thomas K. Glennan, Jr., The Rand Corporation, Santa Monica, and Robert Summers, University of Pennsylvania, Philadelphia.
With 44 illustrations. XIV, 330 pages 8vo. 1967. Cloth DM 56,80; US $ 14.20

RAYMOND H. FOGLER LIBRARY

Q
360
H9